AF784670

# CONTENTS

**February 25, 2004**

## Appendix 2: Additional Material for the Record

# THE CONFLICT BETWEEN SCIENCE AND SECURITY IN VISA POLICY: STATUS AND NEXT STEPS

---

**WEDNESDAY, FEBRUARY 25, 2004**

HOUSE OF REPRESENTATIVES,
COMMITTEE ON SCIENCE,
*Washington, DC.*

The Committee met, pursuant to call, at 9:35 a.m., in Room 2318 of the Rayburn House Office Building, Hon. Sherwood L. Boehlert (Chairman of the Committee) presiding.

# COMMITTEE ON SCIENCE
# U.S. HOUSE OF REPRESENTATIVES

## *The Conflict Between Science and Security in Visa Policy: Status and Next Steps*

Wednesday, February 25, 2004
9:30 a.m. – 12:00 p.m.
2318 Rayburn House Office Building (WEBCAST)

**Witness List**

**The Honorable Asa Hutchinson**
Under Secretary for Border and Transportation Security
Department of Homeland Security

**Mr. Jess Ford**
Director, International Affairs and Trade
General Accounting Office

**Ms. Janice Jacobs**
Deputy Assistant Secretary, Office of Consular Affairs
Department of State

**Mr. Robert Garrity, Jr.**
Deputy Assistant Director, Record/Information Administration
Federal Bureau of Investigation

Section 210 of the Congressional Accountability Act of 1995 applies the rights and protections covered under the Americans with Disabilities Act of 1990 to the United States Congress. Accordingly, the Committee on Science strives to accommodate/meet the needs of those requiring special assistance. If you need special accommodation, please contact the Committee on Science in advance of the scheduled event (3 days requested) at (202) 225-6371 or FAX (202) 225-0891.

Should you need Committee materials in alternative formats, please contact the Committee as noted above.

# THE CONFLICT BETWEEN SCIENCE AND SECURITY IN VISA POLICY: STATUS AND NEXT STEPS

---

# HEARING

BEFORE THE

## COMMITTEE ON SCIENCE
## HOUSE OF REPRESENTATIVES

ONE HUNDRED EIGHTH CONGRESS

SECOND SESSION

---

FEBRUARY 25, 2004

---

**Serial No. 108–43**

---

Printed for the use of the Committee on Science

Available via the World Wide Web: http://www.house.gov/science

U.S. GOVERNMENT PRINTING OFFICE

91–903PS WASHINGTON : 2004

For sale by the Superintendent of Documents, U.S. Government Printing Office
Internet: bookstore.gpo.gov Phone: toll free (866) 512–1800; DC area (202) 512–1800
Fax: (202) 512–2250 Mail: Stop SSOP, Washington, DC 20402–0001

## COMMITTEE ON SCIENCE

HON. SHERWOOD L. BOEHLERT, New York, *Chairman*

RALPH M. HALL, Texas
LAMAR S. SMITH, Texas
CURT WELDON, Pennsylvania
DANA ROHRABACHER, California
KEN CALVERT, California
NICK SMITH, Michigan
ROSCOE G. BARTLETT, Maryland
VERNON J. EHLERS, Michigan
GIL GUTKNECHT, Minnesota
GEORGE R. NETHERCUTT, JR., Washington
FRANK D. LUCAS, Oklahoma
JUDY BIGGERT, Illinois
WAYNE T. GILCHREST, Maryland
W. TODD AKIN, Missouri
TIMOTHY V. JOHNSON, Illinois
MELISSA A. HART, Pennsylvania
J. RANDY FORBES, Virginia
PHIL GINGREY, Georgia
ROB BISHOP, Utah
MICHAEL C. BURGESS, Texas
JO BONNER, Alabama
TOM FEENEY, Florida
RANDY NEUGEBAUER, Texas
VACANCY

BART GORDON, Tennessee
JERRY F. COSTELLO, Illinois
EDDIE BERNICE JOHNSON, Texas
LYNN C. WOOLSEY, California
NICK LAMPSON, Texas
JOHN B. LARSON, Connecticut
MARK UDALL, Colorado
DAVID WU, Oregon
MICHAEL M. HONDA, California
BRAD MILLER, North Carolina
LINCOLN DAVIS, Tennessee
SHEILA JACKSON LEE, Texas
ZOE LOFGREN, California
BRAD SHERMAN, California
BRIAN BAIRD, Washington
DENNIS MOORE, Kansas
ANTHONY D. WEINER, New York
JIM MATHESON, Utah
DENNIS A. CARDOZA, California
VACANCY
VACANCY
VACANCY

HEARING CHARTER

# COMMITTEE ON SCIENCE
# U.S. HOUSE OF REPRESENTATIVES

# The Conflict Between Science and Security in Visa Policy: Status and Next Steps

WEDNESDAY, FEBRUARY 25, 2004
9:30 A.M.–12:00 P.M.
2318 RAYBURN HOUSE OFFICE BUILDING

## 1. Purpose

On Wednesday, February 25, 2004, the House Science Committee will hold a hearing to review the impact of enhanced security measures on the entry into the U.S. of foreign students and scholars. More specifically, the Committee will examine whether the new security measures have enhanced security, whether they have been unnecessarily detrimental to the U.S. scientific enterprise, and how they can be implemented more smoothly. As part of the hearing, the General Accounting Office (GAO) will release a new study, conducted at the Committee's request, on the extent of visa delays and what might be done to reduce them without compromising security.

The hearing will build on a hearing the Committee held on visa issues on March 26, 2003 and on other hearings the Committee has held over the past two years on the impact of security concerns on scientific research.

## 2. Witnesses

**The Honorable Asa Hutchinson** is the Under Secretary for Border and Transportation Security at the Department of Homeland Security (DHS). Prior to being confirmed as Under Secretary, Mr. Hutchinson served as Administrator of the Drug Enforcement Administration. Before that, he served as a Member of Congress from Arkansas from 1997–2001.

**Mr. Jess Ford** is the Director of International Affairs and Trade at the General Accounting Office (GAO). Since 1973, Mr. Ford has worked extensively in the national security and international affairs areas at GAO, with issues ranging from trade, foreign assistance, and foreign policy.

**Ms. Janice Jacobs** is the Deputy Assistant Secretary for the Office of Consular Affairs at the Department of State. Prior to this appointment, she served two years as Deputy Chief of Mission at the U.S. Embassy in Santo Domingo. Ms. Jacobs's 23-year foreign service career has included a mix of Washington, D.C. and overseas assignments, including the Dominican Republic, Ecuador, Egypt, Ethiopia, France, Mexico, Nigeria, and Thailand.

**Mr. Robert Garrity, Jr.** is the Deputy Assistant Director for Record/Information Administration at the Federal Bureau of Investigation (FBI). Mr. Garrity began his career with the FBI in August 1976 and he served in the Savannah, New York, and Dallas field offices. More recently, Mr. Garrity served as the FBI's Interim Records Officer at FBI headquarters, where he was charged with the responsibility of assessing the FBI's records management systems.

## 3. Overarching Questions

- How can the Federal Government implement a visa regime that protects the Nation from terrorist threats without turning away the foreign students and scholars on which the U.S. scientific enterprise has long depended? Have changes in visa processes instituted since September 11th had unnecessary detrimental effects on the U.S. scientific enterprise?
- Does the U.S. collect the data needed to determine the impact of visa processes on the interest and ability of foreign students and scholars to work in the U.S.? Does the U.S. collect the data needed to determine whether visa processes are effectively screening applicants to identify potential terrorists?

- How can the visa processes for foreign students and scholars be made to work more smoothly? Specifically: How does the Administration plan to respond to the new GAO report, just completed for the Science Committee, *Improvements Needed to Reduce Time Taken to Adjudicate Visas for Science Students and Scholars?* What is the current status of the Student Exchange and Visitor Information System (SEVIS), the relatively new, automated and sometimes-troubled system run by DHS to track foreign students in the U.S.? What is the status of the Interagency Panel on Advanced Science Security (IPASS), an interagency committee that was supposed to screen foreign students interested in studying topics that raised security concerns?

### 4. Background and Current Issues

*How dependent is the U.S. scientific enterprise on foreign students and scholars?*

The U.S. has long been a magnet for foreign-born scientists and engineers, and many of the greatest U.S. scientific achievements have depended on them. Two classic examples are the scientists who fled the Nazis before World War II and became the leaders of the program that built the atomic bomb, and the scientists who left Germany after the war and helped form the core of the U.S. space program.

Even with a far more extensive U.S. scientific enterprise today, the U.S. depends on foreign students and scholars. In 1999, the latest year for which figures were available, foreign students received more than one-third of the doctorates awarded in the U.S., and accounted for an even higher percentage in critical scientific fields. Foreign students were awarded almost half the U.S. doctorates in engineering, 47 percent of the doctorates in mathematics and computer sciences, and 40 percent of the doctorates in the physical sciences. Of the foreign students who received doctoral degrees in the U.S., 36 percent came from China and India. Many of them remained in the U.S. after completing their studies. In 1999, 72 percent of foreign doctoral recipients planned to stay in the U.S., and half had already received firm job offers. (Statistics are from National Science Foundation, Science and Engineering Indicators.)

Statistics are not available for faculty, but many faculty in the physical sciences and engineering are also in the U.S. on visas. Also, foreign scholars require visas to attend scientific conferences in the U.S. where their contributions can help U.S. scientists keep abreast of the most important global developments in their fields.

*What changes have taken place since the September 11th attacks that affect foreign students and scholars?*

While the U.S. has benefited incalculably from being a haven for foreign students and scholars, U.S. openness also makes the Nation more vulnerable to security threats. Several of the September 11th hijackers were in the U.S. on student visas (though not to study science or engineering), and scientific know-how gained in the U.S. could later be turned against our country. With that in mind, both Congress and the Administration have made significant changes to the visa system in the past few years. Changes in visa policy and the specific ways those changes have been implemented have tended to make the visa process slower and more cumbersome. The most significant changes are described below:

*New Bureaucracy*

First, in the Act creating the Department of Homeland Security (DHS), Congress significantly altered the bureaucracy in charge of visas. DHS (rather than the State Department) is now in charge of establishing visa policy and reviewing its implementation. The State Department continues to implement the policy by managing consular officers, making decisions on individual visa applications and issuing the visas. The Act also abolished the Immigration and Naturalization Service (INS), which was part of the Justice Department, and replaced it with the Bureau of Immigration and Customs Enforcement (ICE), which is part of DHS. That Bureau is responsible for the student tracking system (SEVIS) and related policies. DHS began full operations last March and has since signed a Memorandum of Understanding with the State Department concerning visa processes.

*Additional Security Checks*

Second, visa applicants are much more likely than they were before September 11th to be subject to security checks. However, the government does not seem to have clear and consistent criteria about which visa applicants warrant a security check or how to determine whether an applicant presents a security threat. The State Department has been encouraging consular officers to err on the side of caution. By contrast, prior to September 11th, State Department visa operations focused primarily on screening applicants to determine whether they intended to work or reside illegally in the U.S. following expiration of their visas rather than on security concerns. Consular officers were encouraged to facilitate legitimate travel, and many even faced pressure to issue more visas.

The security check process for those engaged in sensitive technologies is known as Visas Mantis (Appendix I). Consular officers can request a Visas Mantis review whenever they have doubts about an individual applicant. A request for a Visas Mantis review is sent from the consulate to Washington, and then an investigation is carried out by the FBI or other relevant security agency. State Department officials in Washington review the results of the investigation and advise the consular officer on whether to grant the visa. But the ultimate decision is left up to the consular officer who originally requested the Visas Mantis review.

In deciding whether to request a Visas Mantis review, a consular officer may consider whether a visa applicant will be dealing with technologies that are on the State Department's Technology Alert List (TAL). The TAL includes technologies with potential "dual-use" applications in 15 categories, which range from munitions and rockets to urban planning and sensors. Some observers believe that the TAL is not sufficiently selective to be of real use and increases the likelihood that consular offices will seek Visas Mantis reviews that are not needed. The TAL is so broad that it includes nearly every possible associated technology or skill involving chemistry, biochemistry, immunology, chemical engineering and pharmacology to name a few.

*Personal Interviews*

Third, in August 2003, the State Department issued a new policy, requiring virtually all visa applicants to be interviewed in person by a consular officer. The requirement can only be waived for a person who is either very young or very old. Limited exceptions also exist for diplomatic or official visas and those in the national interest. No additional funds were provided to consulates to meet this additional workload. Delays in scheduling interviews have, in some cases, made it impossible for a student to enroll.

*SEVIS*

Finally, to improve the tracking of foreign students and scholars, Congress created the Student and Exchange Visitor Information System (SEVIS), a computerized database of foreign students in the U.S., which was fully implemented in August 2003. Institutions of higher education must input information on their foreign students into the system and must keep such information as a student's address and educational status up-to-date. SEVIS replaced a paper-based system, which was widely criticized as antiquated and inadequate. Initially, the system was plagued with technical flaws. The system sometimes lost, changed or misplaced data. Universities report that the system is improving, but continues to have technical glitches that may complicate a foreign student's ability to enter the U.S.

*What impact have the new rules had on the U.S. scientific enterprise?*

There are some early indications that the new visa rules are discouraging foreign students from coming to the U.S., and there are numerous anecdotes of students and researchers needlessly running afoul of the new rules, with damage to their research as a result.

According to a recent report by the Institute of International Education, the number of foreign students enrolled in American colleges and universities rose by 0.6 percent in 2002, the smallest growth since 1996. In each of the previous two academic years, foreign student enrollment increased by 6.4 percent. In a 2003 survey of 320 U.S. university officials by the Association of International Education (a different group from the Institute), 94 percent of respondents said they believed that foreign student enrollment was declining because the students felt that U.S. visas were too difficult to get. The drop is coming as other nations are competing more aggressively for students from outside their borders. In the 2003 survey, 45 percent of the university officials said that increased marketing efforts by other countries or relaxation of other countries' visa regulations had contributed to the drop off in foreign students.

Typical of the anecdotes was a case in which a graduate student briefly returned to China after working at the Johns Hopkins Medical School for two years. When he attempted to return to the U.S. he was delayed and his diabetes research was compromised.

*How much information do we have on how the new system is working?*

Data on how the visa system is working is extremely difficult to obtain. The State Department keeps very few statistics related to visas for scientists and engineers.

Also, some information is inherently difficult to obtain, such as information on how many individuals decided not to apply for a visa because of the new regulations.

Broad data can be pieced together. Based on an analysis of State Department data, GAO determined that in fiscal year 2003, the State Department issued 235,579 student visas (for students in all fields and at all levels of study) and 283,660 exchange visitor visas. In that same period, the State Department rejected 128,660 applicants for student visas (for any reason) and 54,614 applicants for exchange visitor visas. No further breakdowns of those data are available.

For example, the State Department has no data on the number of science student and scholar visa applicants who undergo a Visas Mantis check or on how long it took to conduct Visas Mantis checks.

*What did the GAO examination of the system find?*

Because of the lack of data, the Science Committee turned to GAO to get some sense of how the visa system has been working. The study focused on implementation rather than policy. Last March, Science Committee Chairman Boehlert and then-Ranking Member Hall sent a letter to GAO (Appendix II), asking GAO to determine how long it took a science student or scholar from another country to obtain a visa. The request also asked GAO to identify the factors that contributed to visa delays and to review the measures underway to improve the visa process.

*Findings*

GAO reviewed the State Department's visa-related data systems and determined they could not track science applicants within student (F) and exchange visitor (J) visa categories. As a result, they were unable determine the length of time to adjudicate visas for science students or scholars. However, GAO did find that visa adjudication time is largely dependent on whether applicants were subject to Visas Mantis reviews. GAO then sampled Visas Mantis cases involving science students and scholars and determined the following:

- It took an average of 67 days to adjudicate Visas Mantis requests (from the time American consular office received the visa application to the time the Department of State notifies the office of the results of the review).
- Personal interviews with consular officers also contributed to visa delays (generally taking two to three weeks at American consulates in China, India and Russia).
- Many consular staff were concerned that they were contributing to the wait because they lacked clear guidance on when to seek Visas Mantis checks and on whether the checks provided enough background information.

In response to the GAO findings, the Department of State and the FBI reported that they have several measures underway to improve the visa process. To improve transparency, both agencies have set up public inquiry desks to answer questions about the status of pending visa applications. To reduce the time it takes to process Visas Mantis cases, the agencies indicated that they are working together on a case-by-case basis to identify and resolve Visas Mantis cases that have been outstanding for several months to a year (estimated at nearly 1,000 cases). In addition, the State Department has invested $1 million to upgrade its technology for transmitting Visas Mantis requests, though the implementation timetable and other details associated with this technology remain unclear.

*Recommendations*

The GAO report recommended that the Secretary of State, in coordination with the FBI Director, and the Secretary of Homeland Security, develop and implement a plan to improve the Visas Mantis process. In developing this plan, GAO urged the Secretary to consider actions to: 1) establish milestones to reduce the current number of pending Visas Mantis cases; 2) develop performance goals and measurements for processing Visas Mantis checks; 3) provide additional information, through training or other means at consular posts, to clarify guidance on the overall operation of the Visas Mantis program, including when Mantis clearances are required, what information consular posts should submit to enable the clearance process to proceed as efficiently as possible, and how long the process takes; and 4) work to achieve inter-operable systems and expedite transmittal of data between agencies.

*What are the other main problems and issues facing the visa system right now?*

There are a number of issues beyond those discussed above:

*IPASS*

In May 2002, the White House announced that an interagency committee would be set up to review the visa applications of individuals intending to come to the U.S.

as graduate students, post-doctoral fellows, or researchers in "sensitive" fields to do work "uniquely available" on U.S. campuses. The committee was dubbed the Interagency Panel on Advanced Science Security (IPASS) and was to include representatives of the White House Office of Science and Technology Policy (OSTP), DHS, the State Department and other relevant agencies. Initially, OSTP was heading up the efforts to create IPASS, but that task moved to DHS once that Department was created.

DHS is still putting together IPASS. It remains unclear exactly who will be on IPASS, how it will function, and what visa applications it will review. The initial impetus for IPASS was to ensure that federal officials with scientific expertise would have a role in reviewing visas, in part, to prevent foreign scientists from being turned away needlessly. But now, some in the scientific community are concerned that IPASS could add another level of screening and delay to an already burdensome process.

*Visa Waiver*

The Enhanced Border Security Act of 2001 called for 27 countries whose citizens do not require a visa to enter the U.S. (such as Canada, Germany, Britain and New Zealand) to issue passports with biometric data for all citizens who travel to the U.S. Under the law, if one of those countries does not issue such passports by October 26, 2004, then the U.S. will begin requiring visas for that country. So far, only two nations seem likely to meet the deadline. That could mean that the State Department may need to begin processing as many as five million more visa applications annually. That could easily overwhelm the resources of the visa system.

*US VISIT*

The Border Security Act of 2002 requires all U.S. ports of entry to have equipment and software installed that will allow biometric comparison and the authentication of all visas and other travel and entry documents by October 26, 2004. Named the U.S. Visitor and Immigrant Status Indicator Technology (U.S. VISIT) Program by DHS, the system is designed to secure the border and track visa overstays. U.S. VISIT is going to be implemented in phases over the next several years. The first phase has been deployed at 115 airports and 14 seaports. Foreign visitors who require a visa to travel to the U.S., including those in this country on student or exchange visitor visas, will have their travel documents scanned, fingerprints and photos taken, and identification checked against terrorist watch lists. They system replaces the current National Security Entry-Exit Registration System and will be integrated with SEVIS. Some are concerned that the system will not be prepared to handle its first mass influx of students this fall, which could result in delays in entry into the U.S.

*SEVIS*

Although SEVIS continues to improve, a fully functioning system appears to still be a few years away. In addition, in October 2003, the State Department issued a proposed rule to implement the Congressional requirement that the SEVIS system be funded by visa applicants. Universities have a number of concerns about the proposal.

Under the proposed rule, individuals interested in obtaining a visa would have to pay a $100 fee before they are eligible to get a visa application. The fee must be remitted either by credit card or with a check or money order in dollars drawn on a U.S. bank. Universities are concerned that the fee may be too high, that it must be paid even by applicants who do not end up enrolling in a U.S. institution (and only such students get recorded in SEVIS), and that it will create a system of paper receipts that could further slow down the electronic SEVIS system.

**5. Questions for Witnesses**

*Under Secretary Hutchinson (DHS)*

- When establishing visa policy, how do you balance the potential threat of terrorism posed by visiting students and scholars and the benefits to the U.S. of welcoming visiting scholars to participate in our scientific enterprise?
- Is it possible to design a system that will weed out potential terrorists without discouraging the world's best scientists and brightest students from visiting the U.S. and contributing to our knowledge base?
- How does the Department of Homeland Security work with State Department consular officers to help them determine which would-be visiting scholars pose a potential security threat?

- An effective tracking system is an essential tool in reducing the threat of terrorism, yet at a March 2003 Science Committee hearing, one witness testified that the Student and Exchange Visitor Information System (SEVIS) was deployed before it was fully operational, leading to numerous glitches and breaches of confidentiality. What is the current status of SEVIS? What steps has the Department of Homeland Security taken to address problems that were identified last year?
- Is the SEVIS fee a processing fee or a tracking fee? What is the status of the SEVIS fee? How will it be collected and why is that agency best suited for the job? What impact will this method of collection have on foreign students and scholars seeking entry to the U.S.?
- In remarks to the American Association of Universities, Secretary Ridge characterized the Interagency Panel on Advance Science and Security (IPASS) as "one of the greatest solutions" in dealing with the problems of foreign students and scientists. What is the status of IPASS? How will it work? When will it be operational?

*Mr. Garrity (FBI)*

- How are Visas Mantis requests currently transmitted from the State Department to the FBI and from the FBI to the State Department?
- What is your internal process for tracking a Visas Mantis case? How often is that information available electronically? And how often must that file be located physically? What are your plans to fully automate this process? Have there been cases where a file has not been located and the applicant is still pending a response?
- What priority do Visas Mantis investigations have among other FBI work? How do you think these waits impact your ability, and the ability of other law enforcement agencies, to identify and capture a terrorist as opposed to simply preventing him or her from entering the country at that particular post?
- What steps are you taking to make FBI's systems inter-operable with the State Department, which recently invested about $1 million to upgrade its technology for transmitting Visas Mantis requests? Until systems are inter-operable, how will information be transmitted and what impact will it have on processing time?
- How satisfied are you about the appropriateness of the cases referred for additional review under Mantis? Are consular officers providing agents with enough information and the right type of information in their requests?
- What steps have you taken to improve the visa application vetting process? In light of the fact that there have been lengthy waits and there are still Mantis cases that have been pending more than 60 days, what measures do you have underway that will identify and resolve these cases?

*Ms. Jacobs (State)*

- In managing the visa application process, the consular corps, and their functions, how does the State Department balance the potential threat of terrorism posed by visiting students and scholars and the benefits to the U.S. of welcoming visiting scholars to participate in our scientific enterprise?
- In your view, is it possible to design a system that will weed out potential terrorists without discouraging the world's best scientists and brightest students from visiting the U.S. and contributing to our knowledge base?
- What guidance do you provide to consular staff on the Visas Mantis process? Do you provide guidance on when to apply Visas Mantis? How do consular officers know if they are applying the checks appropriately?
- What steps has the State Department taken to improve the visa process during the last year? In light of the fact that there are still Mantis cases that have been pending more than 60 days, what measures do you have underway that will identify and resolve these cases? How do you propose to better track these cases in the future?
- How—and how often—are the results of name checks for Visas Mantis cases provided to the State Department? Why do you think it took the State Department two weeks or longer to inform a post that it could issue a visa?
- What impact have new requirements, such as the personal appearance requirement, had on the length of time it takes to adjudicate a visa? What im-

pact has your request to give priority consideration to students and exchange visitors been accommodated at various posts and how has this impacted staffing? What impact will the implementation of new biometrics requirements in October 2004 have on the length of time to adjudicate a visa?

**Appendix I—Visa Adjudication Process**

1. The process begins when an applicant schedules a visa interview at an American consulate abroad.
2. After receiving an interview time, the applicant goes to the post, where the visa application is reviewed by the consular officer and the applicant's name is checked against the Department of State's automated system of law enforcement watch lists (also known as CLASS).
3. The consular officer reviews the data and conducts a personal interview.
4. If the consular officer determines that the applicant is eligible for non-immigrant status under the INA[1], the applicant moves to the next step in the process. If the applicant is not eligible for non-immigrant status, the visa application is denied.
5. After establishing the applicant's non-immigrant status, the consular officer determines if there is any reason the applicant might be ineligible to receive a visa. After looking to see if the applicant's field or area of study falls under the Technology Alert List (TAL), a consular officer may use his or her discretion to request a security advisory opinion (in the case of TAL, or sensitive technology concerns, this request is known as Visas Mantis).
6. If the consular officer does not request a security advisory opinion, he or she makes a decision to issue or deny a visa to an applicant. If the consular officer requests the security advisory opinion, he or she sends a Visas Mantis cable to State Department headquarters in Washington, DC.
7. The State Department's Consular Affairs sends the cable to the Nonproliferation Bureau, the Federal Bureau of Investigation and other federal agencies.
8. These agencies conduct an investigation and return with their findings to Consular Affairs.
9. Consular Affairs summarizes the findings and returns the prepared security advisory opinion, which indicates whether or not they have an objection to the visa, to posts.
10. Using the security advisory opinion, the consular officer issues or denies the visa to the applicant.

[1] The term non-immigrant generally refers to a foreign national seeking to enter the U.S. temporarily for one of the specified purposes allowed under the Immigration and Nationality Act (INA). The most common reason for denial of a visa is that the applicant intends to come to the U.S. and remain. Section 214(b) of the INA presumes that every alien is an immigrant until he or she establishes that he or she is eligible to non-immigrant status under the INA. Often, this means establishing, in addition to other criteria, that the alien has sufficient social or economic ties to compel him or her to return home after visiting the U.S.

**Appendix II—GAO Request**

The Honorable David M. Walker
Comptroller General of the United States

Dear Comptroller General Walker:

Each year, thousands of international scholars and students participate in education and exchange programs at U.S. universities and institutions. Their research is important to achieving technological advancements that serve U.S. and global interests. Furthermore, it brings together the U.S. and international communities, promoting dialogue and teamwork that is useful for our overall science and foreign policy goals. While the Committee wants to facilitate this type of exchange, we are well aware of the need to balance that effort with those to screen out visa applicants who pose a threat to our country.

We have received information that the research and study plans of some scientific scholars and students from abroad have been derailed because their visa applications were denied or the adjudication process took too long. The Committee believes that it is in our national interest for these visa decisions to be made as quickly as possible, consistent with immigration law and homeland security concerns. For that reason, we would like to obtain a fuller understanding of the visa backlog issue and its magnitude.

We read with interest your report entitled *BORDER SECURITY: Visa Process Should Be Strengthened as an Anti-terrorism Tool.* In particular, we were interested in the report's discussion of the Visas Condor program and the delays and problems identified in the special visa checks initiated after September 11, 2001.

We believe that a similar assessment of the visa process as it pertains to foreign scientific scholars and students (particularly for F–1 and J–1 visas) would be very useful to the Committee and our oversight agenda. In carrying out this investigation, we suggest that you consider (1) results of visa adjudication, including denial rates, visa backlogs, and duration of visa reviews, (2) operation of the Visas Mantis program, (3) visa policies and procedures concerning applicants who will engage in research or studies involving potentially sensitive technologies, (4) existing exchange programs and bilateral protocols guiding scientific exchanges, and (5) the impact of actions taken since September 11 to strengthen and improve visa policies and procedures.

In addition, because many seeking entry to the United States for scientific research and studies are citizens of China (mainland and Taiwan), India and Russia, we ask that you determine what other factors may be affecting the processing of visas in these countries, including adequacy of trained staff at post, level of scrutiny over applications, and special security or other concerns.

Based on your analysis, we would appreciate your thoughts on potential improvements that can be made. As you develop your work scope, please contact Kara Haas at 225–8115 to discuss study alternatives and timing.

Thank you for the kind consideration of this request. We look forward to your findings.

Sincerely,

Sherwood Boehlert
Chairman

Ralph Hall
Ranking Member

**Appendix III—Request for Written Testimony from Dr. Marburger**

John H. Marburger, III, Ph.D.
Director
Office of Science and Technology Policy
Executive Office of the President
Washington, DC 20502

Dear Dr. Marburger:

I understand that you will be unable to attend the Science Committee's February 25 hearing on the impact of new visa regulations on the ability of foreign students and scholars to enroll in education and engage in research in the U.S. Your perspective on this issue is important, however, and I would appreciate it if you could provide written answers to the following questions by February 20, 2004.

1. The Office of Science and Technology Policy (OSTP), together with the Office of Homeland Security, established an interagency working group to implement the requirements of Homeland Security Presidential Directive 2, which called on the Federal Government to prohibit certain international students from receiving education and training in sensitive areas. In May 2002, based on the recommendations of the working group, the White House unveiled its plan to create an Interagency Panel on Advanced Science Security (IPASS) to provide increased scrutiny for student or exchange visitor applicants who hoped to study or conduct research in certain sensitive science and technology fields. What is the status of IPASS? When will IPASS be operational?
2. What role does OSTP currently have in IPASS?
3. When you appeared before the Science Committee in October 2002, you indicated that those responsible for the enhanced review of sensitive science and technology under IPASS would be drawn from the Department of State, the Immigration and Naturalization Service (U.S. Citizenship and Immigration Bureau, Department of Homeland Security), intelligence and law enforcement agencies, and federal science and technology agencies. What role have you—or the federal science and technology agencies under your purview—had in the review of the visa applications of science students and scholars? Does this structure meaningfully enhance homeland security or stem the proliferation of sensitive science and technology without the case-by-case review by scientific experts envisioned by IPASS? Absent IPASS, how can we embed technical expertise in the visa process?
4. In what way is your Office monitoring the extent to which security procedures are hampering the entry of scientists and engineers to the United States? Have you pressed for additional data collection so that policy-makers can get a clearer picture of the impact of the security regime?

Thank you for addressing these issues. It is my hope that this hearing will encourage greater cooperation among the various agencies involved in the visa process—and provide greater appreciation for the impact of visa delays on students, scientists, universities and research facilities.

Sincerely,

SHERWOOD BOEHLERT
Chairman

Chairman BOEHLERT. I want to welcome everyone to this morning's hearing which focuses on two issues of vital concern to this committee, and to the Nation as a whole; namely, how to enhance homeland security and how to ensure that we continue to have a thriving scientific enterprise. When it comes to visa policy, we sometimes talk about finding the proper balance between those two concerns. But talk of balance is in many ways misleading. Our nation will not be secure in the long run if it does not have a healthy scientific enterprise, and science cannot thrive in an atmosphere of insecurity.

But security and science are also complementary in more practical ways that must be kept in mind when reviewing visa policy. A visa regime that casts too wide a net that holds up just about everybody for excessive security checks, that regime is not good for security or for science. It is not good for security because it distracts and overwhelms the system, taking resources away from investigations of individuals more likely to present a real threat to our nation. And it is obviously not good for science, given that the United States' success in science has always depended on attracting the best minds from around the world.

Now all of this is easier to talk about in the abstract than to implement on a daily basis. Potential terrorists obviously aren't easily identifiable. As a Member of the Intelligence Committee, I am painfully aware of the real and insidious threats facing our nation. I spent three hours yesterday afternoon with the Director of the CIA in a world threat assessment briefing. Not very comforting. In the immediate wake of September 11, it was right to err on the side of caution. But we have had time to learn since then and we can't have a visa system that needlessly discourages and alienates scientists from around the world who could be a boon to this country.

The General Accounting Office study that Congressman Hall and I requested, and that will be released at this hearing, indicates that we have some real problems with our current visa processes. That shouldn't surprise anyone. The study also indicates that we can solve these problems without compromising security, and in that respect, let me compliment one of our witnesses, Secretary Hutchinson, for the leadership he is providing in this area.

I know about the problems, not only from the fine work of GAO, but from personal experience. I had to personally intervene repeatedly to get a visa for Dr. Ramon Bruguda, a world-class heart specialist who was featured recently in the *New York Times* for his life-saving research. He was having trouble getting permission to come to this country to do his world-class research at the Masonic Research Facility in my hometown of Utica, New York. Our visa system shouldn't be spending its time worrying about the Ramon Brugudas of the world.

I am very pleased and grateful that we have before us today my friend and former colleague, Secretary Hutchinson, who is the person on the hot seat on this issue. His job ain't easy. Secretary Hutchinson has the extraordinarily daunting task of creating a visa policy that will let in scientists, while keeping out terrorists. I look forward to hearing from him. I hope that at the end of this hearing, we will have reached at least a preliminary agreement on steps that can be taken to make sure that our consular officers ask for security checks on anyone who might present a threat, but only on those who might present a threat, and how to collect better data to see if our visa security processes are properly focused.

Everyone has to be willing to put up with more delays and bureaucracy in the post-September 11 world. But we still have an obligation to ensure that we are not needlessly alienating scholars from around the world who could help this Nation, and that we are not unnecessarily hamstringing or burdening our universities and research centers. As I said earlier in my testimony, and my high school English teacher would be offended if she heard me say it, it ain't easy. This is very, very difficult, and we all have to be mindful of the challenge facing Secretary Hutchinson and Governor Ridge. It is a difficult task.

Our purpose here is to work cooperatively to face that challenge and overcome it in a responsible way so that we can shape public policy to the benefit of all Americans. Mr. Gordon.

[The prepared statement of Chairman Boehlert follows:]

PREPARED STATEMENT OF CHAIRMAN SHERWOOD BOEHLERT

I want to welcome everyone to this morning's hearing, which focuses on two issues of vital concern to this committee and to the Nation as a whole—namely, how to enhance homeland security and how to ensure that we continue to have a thriving scientific enterprise.

When it comes to visa policy, we sometimes talk about finding "the proper balance" between those two concerns. But talk of balance is in many ways misleading. Our nation will not be secure, in the long run, if it does not have a healthy scientific enterprise, and science cannot thrive in an atmosphere of insecurity.

But security and science are also complementary in more practical ways that must be kept in mind when reviewing visa policy. A visa regime that casts too wide a net—that holds up just about everybody for excessive security checks—that regime is not good for security or for science.

It's not good for security because it distracts and overwhelms the system, taking resources away from investigations of individuals more likely to present a real threat to our nation. And it's obviously not good for science, given that U.S. success in science has always depended on attracting the best minds from around the world.

Now all this is easier to talk about in the abstract than to implement on a daily basis. Potential terrorists obviously aren't easily identifiable. As a Member of the Intelligence Committee, I'm painfully aware of the real and insidious threats facing our nation. And in the immediate wake of September 11th, it was right to err on the side of caution.

But we've had time to learn since then, and we can't have a visa system that needlessly discourages and alienates scientists from around the world who could be a boon to this country. The General Accounting Office (GAO) study that Congressman Hall and I requested, and that will be released at this hearing, indicates that we have some real problems with our current visa processes. The study also indicates that we can solve those problems without compromising security.

I know about the problems not only from the fine work of GAO, but from personal experience. I had to intervene repeatedly to get a visa for Dr. Ramon Bruguda, a world-class heart specialist, featured recently in *The New York Times* for his life-saving research, who was having trouble getting permission to come to this country to do work at the Masonic Home in Utica. Our visa system shouldn't be spending its time worrying about the Ramon Brugudas of the world.

I'm very pleased and grateful that we have before us today, my friend and former colleague, Secretary Hutchinson, who is the person in the hot seat on this issue. Asa has the extraordinarily daunting task of creating a visa policy that will let in scientists while keeping out terrorists. I look forward to hearing from him.

I hope that at the end of this hearing, we will have reached at least a preliminary agreement on steps that can be taken to make sure that our consular officers ask for security checks on anyone who might present a threat, but only on those who might present a threat, and on how to collect better data to see if our visa security processes are properly focused.

Everyone has to be willing to put up with more delays and bureaucracy in the post-September 11th world. But we still have an obligation to ensure that we are not needlessly alienating scholars from around the world who could help this nation, and that we are not unnecessarily ham-stringing or burdening our universities and research centers.

Mr. Gordon.

Mr. GORDON. Thank you, Mr. Chairman.

I want to join you in welcoming our witnesses today, and I want to thank you for providing the opportunity for the Committee to explore this important issue. As I was listening to your opening statement, as usual, I concur, and quite frankly could not add to it or make it any better. So I will just again concur with your remarks, and we will move forward.

[The prepared statement of Mr. Gordon follows:]

PREPARED STATEMENT OF REPRESENTATIVE BART GORDON

I am pleased to join the Chairman in welcoming our witnesses to today's hearing.

I want to thank the Chairman for providing this opportunity for the Committee to explore an important issue that is at the intersection of strengthening homeland security and ensuring the well being of the Nation's science and technology enterprise.

Throughout much of our history, the United States has benefited from the infusion of scientific and engineering talent from abroad.

Today, U.S. universities rely on foreign students to fill half or more of their graduate student positions in many fields of science, mathematics and engineering.

Without these students, research programs could not go forward; and since about half of the graduates from these programs remain here, the science and technology capabilities of the Nation would also suffer if this pipeline were to dry up.

As we learned in our hearing last Spring, there is growing evidence that excessive delays and uncertainty in obtaining visas by foreign students and scholars has made the U.S. less attractive as a destination for scientific training and for research collaborations.

While the Nation clearly benefits from the presence of international students and scholars, we all understand the importance of being vigilant in guarding our boarders against those who would do us harm.

Putting in place effective screening procedures for visa applications is reasonable and necessary.

The issue before us today is not whether we need thorough and effective procedures for reviewing visa applications. Rather it is to find an appropriate balance between two important national goals.

On the one hand we benefit from attracting talented international students to our universities, and we benefit by nurturing scientific collaborations and information exchange with foreign researchers.

On the other hand, we must defend ourselves against terrorists.

We must find ways to ensure that boarder security is applied effectively while also ensuring that this country remains an inviting place for bright foreign students to study and for scientific exchanges to occur with leading researchers from all parts of the world.

The Committee charged the GAO to explore the current state of the visa application and approval process to help us understand how well it is working and to make recommendations on how it could be improved.

The GAO's recommendations focus on the need for the three agencies represented here today to work together to develop and implement an improvement plan for the Visas Mantis process—the main source of delay in the processing of visas for science applicants.

I look forward to hearing the agencies' reactions to the GAO findings and recommendations regarding the sticking points in the system, and how it can be made to work better.

Also, I hope to learn what has become of the Interagency Panel on Advanced Science and Security, which Secretary Ridge has characterized as one of the greatest solutions for dealing with visa requests by students and scientists.

I want to thank the Chairman for calling a hearing on this important subject.

I appreciate the attendance of our witnesses today, and I look forward to our discussion.

Thank you and yield back.

Chairman BOEHLERT. Thank you very much. Mr. Smith, do you have any opening remarks? Thank you very much.
[The prepared statement of Mr. Costello follows:]

PREPARED STATEMENT OF REPRESENTATIVE JERRY F. COSTELLO

Good morning. I want to thank the witnesses for appearing before our committee to discuss the impact of security measures to control entry of foreign students and scholars into the United States. I believe we must work hard to balance national security with the needs of universities. If visa delays and denials are indeed substantially increasing, the U.S. science and technology enterprise could be damaged.

In response to events such as the 1993 World Trade Center bombing and the attacks of September 11, 2001, concerns have been raised about foreign students in the U.S. as well as the courses they studied and research they conducted. Certain government officials and members of the intelligence community were concerned that our existing student visa policy and free learning environment would provide terrorists easy access to our country and put us at risk of training future terrorists in sensitive areas. New regulations were imposed on processing visa applications, which have caused severe backlogs, delays, denials, and has hindered attendance at international conferences. Universities depend heavily on foreign students to fill postgraduate programs, particularly in science, and these students represent an important source of research assistance in the sciences and mathematics. In engineering, foreign students make up half of all candidates for advanced degrees. While national security is a great concern, we must recognize that very few international students are indeed a risk to the U.S. and the vast majority provides necessary assistance to our nation's academic environment.

In my congressional district, Southern Illinois University–Carbondale has been experiencing delays and decreases in international enrollments. Grassroots efforts have been underway to bring attention to the issue. For example, the Carbondale City Council recently passed a resolution objecting to certain cumbersome restrictions placed on foreign students. The decline in the international student population has had strong consequences for not only the university but also the town itself. The schools, businesses, and community are all enriched by the international community and are feeling the effects of the delays and decreases.

I am interested to learn more about the trends in delays and denials over the past few years. I am also interested in learning more about implementation of the student visa system policy and ensuring that the overall process is both efficient and effective.

I welcome our panel of witnesses and look forward to their testimony.

[The prepared statement of Ms. Johnson follows:]

PREPARED STATEMENT OF REPRESENTATIVE EDDIE BERNICE JOHNSON

Thank Mr. Chairman, and thank you for calling this hearing today. I would also like to thank our invited guests for appearing.

Today, we meet to examine the new security measures that have been put in place to enhance national security. We all agree that foreign scientists and scholars are important to maintaining the vitality and quality of the U.S. research enterprise. In fact, almost 35 percent of advanced degrees are conferred upon foreign scholars resident in the U.S. for all areas of science and technology.

However, because of the events of September 11, Congress and the Administration took action to track foreign students and more carefully review the applications of those wishing to study sensitive areas of science and technology in the U.S.

But scientists and educators complain that consular officers are using vague, arbitrary standards to decide which visa applications to refer for security reviews, trapping legitimate foreign researchers in a frustrating backlog.

These delays bother educators and scientists, who say the free exchange of ideas is essential to scientific discovery. They point out that foreign-born scientists have been responsible for many major advances in medicine and technology, including the kidney dialysis machine, the Pap smear, plastic and the atomic bomb.

The National Academies (the National Academy of Science, the National Academy of Engineering and the Institute of Medicine) complained over a year ago that recent efforts by the government to constrain the flow of international visitors in the name of national security are having serious unintended consequences for American science, engineering and medicine.

It is a sad day when even the research to combat chemical biological terrorism has been stalled by the visa delays.

In fact, in my home state of Texas, the 44,192 foreign students at colleges and universities fuel Texas' economy with money is spent on tuition and living expenses in excess of $700 million dollar during the 2001–2002 school year alone. Therefore, foreign students are an essential part of our economic structure.

Let me make this clear, educators and scientist support tighter screening of visitors after 9/11. However, something must be done to streamline the visa. I hope our witnesses can shine some light today on possible solutions.

[The prepared statement of Mr. Davis follows:]

PREPARED STATEMENT OF REPRESENTATIVE LINCOLN DAVIS

I would like to echo the comments of the Chairman and Ranking Member as to the great importance of this issue of student visas.

There must be a careful balance between an efficient and effective, homeland security system and a student visa system that doesn't hold up bright, productive researchers from training and contributing to the great scientific research being done in this country.

As we know, some of the 9/11 terrorists took advantage of the student visa system. Everyone in this room has concerns about the way people are admitted into this country. Several Members have introduced bills focusing on security issues. Representative Pete Sessions and I have also introduced a homeland security bill addressing visa issues.

I thank the witnesses who are here today to clear up some of these concerns.

[The prepared statement of Ms. Jackson Lee follows:]

PREPARED STATEMENT OF REPRESENTATIVE SHEILA JACKSON LEE

Mr. Chairman,

Thank you for calling this important and timely hearing. I would also like to welcome this distinguished panel for coming to join us today. Mr. Hutchison, thank you for taking the time from your important work to let us benefit from your insights.

The transition from the pre-9/11 world to the post-9/11 world has presented challenges that Congress will probably be dealing with for years. Making this nation safer will be an ongoing project. Of course the transition will impact our Defense and Intelligence and State Departments. But it will also touch almost every sector of American life—our agriculture, our communications systems, our hospitals—and as we see today our research centers.

American labs lead the world in the biological and physical sciences. We have a rich tradition of openness and collaboration with partners from around the world. The best and the brightest come from all over to attend our fine colleges and universities as students or fellows, or just to attend conferences and symposia. That kind of interaction has many benefits. Our students get exposed to more diverse ideas and opinions, and become more competitive because of it. Our labs get excellent workers for little money. That feeds our industries and our economy. Our scientists are enabled to forge collaborations with scientists around the world that make them more effective.

And, of course, the foreign visitor gets great benefits as well. They get an outstanding education or research experience. Sometimes they end up getting a job here. Often they go home. Regardless, they have a better understanding and appreciation for American people and culture. These days when even our allies find us troubling, and our enemies feel we deserve destruction—that kind of person-to-person diplomacy can be an excellent investment.

But opening up our doors brings risks as well. There are people out there who wish to do us harm, so it is prudent that we do what we can to keep them out. However, the vast majority of people who apply for visas are peaceful. The challenge, therefore, is finding the perfect balance: efficiently welcoming the many lawful visitors into the Nation, while putting in obstacles that are most likely to block would-be terrorists.

Right now, it seems that we have a cumbersome system that penalizes all foreign students, exchange scientists, and our own universities, and probably would not do much good in preventing attacks. As we learned over the past weeks in Pakistan, it is probably much easier to buy weapons technology on the black market than it is to find an intelligent young terrorist "wannabe" and send him to the United States for a five-year Ph.D. or post-doctoral fellowship. It is hard to imagine a few-minute interview with a first-year foreign service person, would stop many terrorists. And the long waiting lists we have now for exchange visas probably serve no one, since I would assume that a good portion of the 2–3 month wait is time that the application sits in an inbox.

I don't mean to be too harsh. I know that all of the agencies are struggling to cope with new challenges in the wake of 9/11. But we must be critical and probing so that we can quickly refine our methods to achieve the best possible balance of openness and security. We need to develop an effective high-throughput system. If we don't we could cripple our scientific progress, and simultaneously leave ourselves vulnerable to terrorists.

That is why I am proud of the initiative taken by this committee in calling for a GAO report on this critical subject. I look forward to hearing from this panel, about how our visa policy is working. I want to know what are the weak links, or the rate-limiting steps in the application process. We all have the same goals here today. I hope that we can work together to make this nation safer, and provide for scientific and cultural growth or years to come.

Thank you.

Chairman BOEHLERT. Our witnesses today are a very distinguished panel, and we want to thank all of you for serving as resources for this committee. We are here to learn, and so we will listen in order to learn, and then we will question and then we will have a meaningful dialogue, hopefully.

The Honorable Asa Hutchinson is the Under Secretary for Border and Transportation Security at the Department of Homeland Security. Prior to being confirmed as Under Secretary, Mr. Hutchinson served as Administrator of the Drug Enforcement Administration (he is a glutton for punishment). Before that, he served as a Member of Congress from Arkansas from 1997 to 2001, and it was our privilege to call him a colleague.

Mr. Jess Ford is Director of International Affairs and Trade at the General Accounting Office. Since 1973, Mr. Ford has worked extensively in the national security and international affairs area at GAO, with issues ranging from trade and foreign assistance, to foreign policy.

Ms. Janice Jacobs is the Deputy Assistant Secretary for the Office of Consular Affairs at the Department of State. Prior to this appointment, she served two years as Deputy Chief of Mission at the U.S. Embassy in Santa Domingo. Ms. Jacobs' 23-year distinguished foreign service career has included a mix of Washington, D.C. and overseas assignments, including the Dominican Republic, Ecuador, Egypt, Ethiopia, France, Mexico, Nigeria and Thailand.

And Mr. Robert Garrity, Jr., is a Deputy Assistant Director for Record/Information Administration at the Federal Bureau of Investigation. Mr. Garrity began his career with the FBI in August 1976, and he served in the Savannah, New York and Dallas field offices. More recently, Mr. Garrity served as the FBI's Interim Records Officer at FBI headquarters, where he was charged with the responsibility of assessing the FBI's records management systems. Quite a challenge.

Lady and gentlemen, it is our privilege to welcome you here. We would ask that you try to summarize your opening statement. This committee is not arbitrary because this is so important, but we try to give you a guideline of five minutes or so. Don't get nervous if the red light comes on if you have got a thought or a paragraph you want to finish.

Mr. Hutchinson, you are up first.

## STATEMENT OF THE HONORABLE ASA HUTCHINSON, UNDER SECRETARY FOR BORDER AND TRANSPORTATION SECURITY, DEPARTMENT OF HOMELAND SECURITY

Mr. HUTCHINSON. Thank you, Mr. Chairman, Ranking Member Gordon. It is a pleasure to be with you, all the Members of the Committee, and I would emphasize at the outset that the Department of Homeland Security agrees with the sentiments expressed by the Chairman on the importance of academic access to the outstanding educational institutions of our nation.

Our goal is to facilitate such access in a way that is consistent with security, and not to impede or deny those opportunities. Higher education is the fifth largest service sector export, and international students contribute $12 billion to the U.S. economy through tuition and general spending. Welcoming foreign scholars, scientists and researchers into our country expands knowledge, fosters a sharing of information, and aids the development of technologies critical to our defense and the defense of our allies.

But as we are all aware, the benefits of this exchange must be protected against exploitation by those who would use that information to threaten our security. Two September 11 terrorists abused the foreign student program to enter and stay in the United States. Since then, actions have been taken. President Bush mandated action to end the abuse of student visas and to prohibit certain international students from receiving education and training in sensitive areas. Likewise, the U.S.A. Patriot Act mandates an electronic system to monitor student and school compliance with immigration laws.

These security directives have been accomplished through SEVIS, the Student and Exchange Visitor Information System. This system electronically tracks the entry and exit of the more than 800,000 international students who visit the United States each year. Despite these security measures, it is not in the interest of the United States to place unnecessary burdens or delays on legitimate foreign students and scientists. One of the subjects of this hearing is the recent GAO report, which I understand will be released today, which identifies some security measures that may cause delays.

Let me just simply address the perspective of homeland security. The Homeland Security Act transferred to the Department of Homeland Security the responsibility for establishing visa policy and to review how these policies are implemented. This authority is exercised in close consultation in cooperation with the Department of State, pursuant to a memorandum of agreement that was signed with the Department of State on September 26 of last year. As a result of this transfer of visa policy, we are working with the Bureau of Consular Affairs in a number of areas. First of all, to improve the visa revocation notification processes. Secondly, we have taken the lead role in the statutorily mandated country reviews of participating Visa Waiver Program nations, and third, we are in the process of establishing the Visa Security Program, as mandated by Congress, which builds on the experience that we are gaining in Saudi Arabia, which is our Visa Security Office. This year, we anticipate opening four additional Visa Security Offices that will add a security perspective on visa issuance, and also hopefully to help facilitate the processing of those visas that are legitimate.

Our staffs are also working to review the special visa application process known as Security Advisory Opinions. Through this, the U.S. Government is able to more closely scrutinize the security implications of issuing visas and permitting the travel of certain individuals. One trigger of the Security Advisory Opinions is the Visas Mantis process. This Visas Mantis is a coordinated procedure between intelligence and border security agencies to determine whether the travel of certain foreign students and business people may jeopardize the safeguarding of critically sensitive technology and information.

Finally, I know a special interest has been expressed by this committee in the SEVIS program and certain technical difficulties that were being experienced by system users at the time of the March 2003 hearing on this subject. The Department has spent a substantial amount of time, resources and personnel to correct these problems, and we have added a number of system corrections to make SEVIS easier to use and to increase compliance. But I think of great significance to this committee is the fact that we created a SEVIS Response Team, anticipating the return of a couple 100,000 foreign students and scholars to the United States, anticipating that there might be some glitches, and wanting to eliminate those glitches so that they are not turned back whenever they are a legitimate student.

We created the Response Team, a personnel investment, whereby an inspector at a port of entry, when they encounter a student that might not be properly entered into the online system, we can then have the inspector call the Response Team. We can then check with the university. Is this person a valid student or not? They fax us the I–20 form. We, while that student is waiting, can get them cleared through. Whenever there is a question but our instinct is that this is a legitimate student, we will waive them in and then have that verified in terms of having the I–20 provided to us.

These teams have responded to more than 8,000 calls, which means we have facilitated over 8,000 scholars and foreign students coming into our educational institutions. During that process, though, we identified over 200 individuals, right at a little over 200, posing as legitimate students. But whenever they did not have their I–20, when they were not registered in the SEVIS online system, we would call and verify with the academic institution, and they would say we have never heard of that student. Those individuals were denied entry into our country and turned away, and I believe that that illustrates the success of the response team, both in terms of facilitating legitimate scholars that come to our schools, welcoming them, but at the same time, adding the security measure that is important to our country.

At this point, SEVIS is a highly capable, reliable system that has accomplished the purpose it was designed for. In the words of the president of the American Counsel of Education, David Ward, "SEVIS is the most important step that the Federal Government can take to improve its ability to monitor international students, scholars and exchange visitors, and we strongly support its full and effective implementation."

I'll end with a comment that we are relying a great deal upon technology. It is important for us to facilitate travel, commerce, education, but at the same time, to zero in on those people that might pose a risk. But despite our investment in technology, the greatest protection are those human resources and a trained workforce that does a good job out there in interviewing and using their judgment and discretion, as they accomplish the security objectives and the educational needs of our society. I look forward to our discussions and questions later.

[The prepared statement of Mr. Hutchinson follows:]

PREPARED STATEMENT OF ASA HUTCHINSON

Mr. Chairman, Members of the Committee:

I appreciate the opportunity to testify before you on the subject of how we can remain a welcoming nation to foreign scholars and scientists and not compromise security requirements. I would emphasize at the outset that the Department of Homeland Security (DHS) appreciates the importance of academic access to the outstanding educational institutions of our nation. Our goal is to facilitate such access in a way that is consistent with security and not to impede or deny those opportunities. Specifically, today, I will speak about those individuals who seek to come to our country to study, research or acquire advanced technologies. The development, knowledge and sharing of information about these advanced technologies are crucial to our defense and the defense of our allies, so there is good reason to permit the entry of foreign scholars, scientists and researchers. However, as we are all aware, when access to these resources and technologies is provided to those who mean us harm, then the security of our nation and that of our allies is compromised. Consequently, we have the responsibility to review and, as needed, establish policies and procedures that permit a more secure way to protect the flow of scientific information and individuals to and from our country. The Homeland Security Act transferred to the Secretary the responsibility to mange policy affecting visa issuance.

As a result of this mandate, on September 26, 2003, Secretary of State Powell and Secretary Ridge signed a Memorandum of Understanding (MOU) that addresses the division of responsibilities between the two departments with regard to visa issuance. As stated in the MOU, the Departments will work together to "create and maintain an effective, efficient visa process that secures America's borders from external threats and ensures that our borders remain open to legitimate travel.. . ." This declaration supports DHS' national strategy and Secretary Powell's vision of "Secure Borders, Open Doors," and affirms the Administration's understanding of the importance of such policy to our international, economic, and national interests, as well as to the security of our homeland.

I would like to mention briefly some of the actions that DHS has already begun taking to enhance border security by evaluating visa issuance policy to identify vulnerabilities and, when possible, to improve the efficiency and effectiveness of the process. We are working with the Department of State's (DOS) Bureau of Consular Affairs on improving the visa revocation and notification processes. Our staffs have also worked closely to restructure the review and processing of requests for waivers of inadmissibility and the special visa application evaluative process, known as "Security Advisory Opinions" (SAOs). I will speak more about SAOs in a moment. The DHS has also taken the lead role in the statutory mandated country reviews of participating Visa Waiver Program nations.

As I mentioned a moment ago, we are beginning to be actively involved in the SAO process by which the U.S. government more closely scrutinizes the effect of issuing visas to and permitting the travel of certain individuals on the security of the country. Of particular importance to the subject of the testimony today is the "Visas Mantis" process. Visas Mantis is a coordinated procedure between intelligence and border security agencies to determine whether the travel of certain foreign students and businessman may jeopardize the safeguarding of critically sensitive technology and information. Understanding the need to balance threats to national security with the need to welcome visiting scholars, DHS is working with DOS to develop policies which will ensure that the impact of the SAO/Visas Mantis processes is reviewed regularly. These policies will articulate and address the need for:

- effective efficient, and consistent procedures;

- regular feedback to post officials, including visa security officers on their application of SAO policy and procedures and their management of SAO cases;
- tracking and integrating visa applications that raise national security concerns into a larger intelligence/security framework; and
- implementing best practices for facilitating the visa issuance and public access to information.

Prior to the establishment of DHS, there was some preliminary development of IPASS, a proposed interagency panel that would scrutinize students and exchange visitor applicants who intended to study certain sensitive science and technology fields. DHS intends to review the Mantis process with the intent of incorporating the best elements of the IPASS concept without creating an additional layer of review.

Furthermore, building on our experience in Saudi Arabia, the Department is also establishing the Visa Security Program (VSP) which will expand DHS' presence at consular posts. Since the implementation of the VSP in Saudi Arabia, DHS has reviewed 100 percent of visa applications at the consular posts there, in compliance with the statutory mandate and is moving forward to refine VSP operations and procedures. The VSP is using the experience in Saudi Arabia as a model for developing its program plans, systems needs and organizational structure. DHS is initially planning to establish the VSP at four additional locations.

I know Committee Members have expressed special interest in SEVIS, and I will now report on its status and current functionality. Witness testimony given at the March 2003 House Science Committee hearing reflected the technical difficulties that were being experienced by system users at that time. However, DHS has addressed and corrected each of the critical system problems that were noted in the March 2003 testimony. In addition to addressing the system problems, DHS has added a large number of system enhancements to SEVIS to increase the ease of system use. These system changes were largely identified by and implemented at the request of system users. While SEVIS is still evolving as a system, it was fully implemented by January 1, 2003, in accordance with the USA PATRIOT Act. System releases following implementation addressed the large majority of system problems, including changes that incorporate the resolution of every anomaly that was discussed in the March 2003 hearing. During Fiscal Years 2003 and 2004, SEVIS will have undergone a total of twelve major releases, which represent several hundred individual improvements. Changes in these releases include the SEVIS–U.S. VISIT interface, enhanced reporting capabilities, especially regarding enforcement-related data, and e-gov software upgrades.

The subsequent successful implementation and expansion of SEVIS has been the direct result of our aggressive effort to analyze anomalies, prioritize remediation, and implement fixes. This series of system changes not only ensures that SEVIS "works as advertised," but also enhances the system to respond to end user needs.

SEVIS implementation and execution requires the partnership of DHS, colleges, universities, exchange visitor programs, and all other organizations and individuals participating in the education of foreign students and exchange visitors in the United States. Through our Internet website, publications, participation in the conferences of professional associations, help desks, and one-on-one communication, the "Student and Exchange Visitor Program" (SEVP) has taken a comprehensive inventory of customer needs and desires.

With regard to suggested reported "breaches of confidentiality," we are aware of only a handful of instances where this may have occurred. Extensive system analysis has revealed that the likelihood of these occurring was one in 40,000 system transactions. However, DHS recognized that even this level was unacceptable and a solution to this inconsistency was implemented in May 2003. No new data crossover issues have been identified since then.

At this point, SEVIS is highly capable, reliable, and more than able to support the purposes for which it was designed. DHS will also continue to address outstanding issues and enhance the system according to system user needs.

SEVIS and SEVP are required to be fully user-fee funded, in accordance with Section 641 of the Illegal Immigration Reform and Immigrant Responsibility Act of 1996 (IIRIRA). Funds were appropriated to the Immigration and Naturalization Service by Congress after September 11th in order to complete the technical development of SEVIS by the mandatory deadline. However, having expended those funds in the accelerated development and deployment of SEVIS, the SEVP must begin collection of the student fee in this fiscal year to continue the program. The projected revenue from the SEVIS fee will provide the funding for the SEVP within the Bureau of Immigration and Customs Enforcement. This includes upgrades and maintenance of the SEVIS database, school liaison officers as well as the monitoring and enforcement functions associated with the program.

The proposed SEVIS fee rule was published in the *Federal Register* on October 27, 2003, with a 60-day comment period ending on December 26, 2003. We are currently working to finalize the rule.

Section 641 of IIRIRA also mandates that the fee be paid prior to visa issuance. DHS has made efforts to reach a workable arrangement for fee collection with the Department of State at the time of visa issuance. However, such an arrangement is not possible at this time. Therefore, the SEVIS rule requires that DHS collect the fee. The fee may be paid by the intending student, a third party of the student's choice, and in some cases in bulk payments made by the sponsoring program. Current options for paying the fee are by check drawn on U.S. funds, by mail, or online with a credit card. In addition, school, sponsoring program, or "third party" payments are allowed and program sponsors can pay for participants via "batch" payment. The SEVP will continue to assess additional payment options, which may be made available at some later date.

Technology systems and solutions alone cannot "weed out" potential terrorists and allow us to identify those scientists, students and businessmen whose contributions would be clearly beneficial to the U.S. Doing so requires the expertise and evaluative abilities of the consular officers, technical and security advisers, and the officers at the Ports of Entry. We must, however, develop policies and procedures and use technologies as tools to allow all involved individuals to make proper and more informed judgments. And while I predict that technology will play a critical role in defending us against further harm, I must also acknowledge that our best defense is a well-trained and resourced workforce.

And lastly while the ultimate responsibility for our national security rests with the public sector we should and must recognize that industry and academia play critical roles in ensuring that our most valuable technological and intellectual assets are protected and secured by developing and implementing practices which assist the overall security of our nation and our allies. While I have the primary responsibility in DHS for visa policy, I have worked, and will continue to work closely, with Under Secretary Charles McQuery of DHS' Science and Technology Directorate to ensure that the concerns of scientists and engineers are adequately addressed.

I would be please to take any questions at this time.

### Biography for Asa Hutchinson

Asa Hutchinson was appointed by President Bush and confirmed by a unanimous vote of the U.S. Senate in January 2003.

As Under Secretary for Border and Transportation Security, Hutchinson leads a directorate of over 110,000 employees and is responsible for coordinating the enforcement activities of our borders, transportation and immigration systems.

Prior to coming to DHS, Hutchinson served as a Member of Congress from Arkansas from 1997–2001. While in Congress, Hutchinson served on the Select Committee on Intelligence and the House Judiciary Committee.

After being re-elected to his third term, he was appointed as Administrator of the Drug Enforcement Administration (DEA), where he combined tough law enforcement initiatives with advocating increased investment in treatment and education programs.

Prior to his election to Congress, Hutchinson practiced law in rural Arkansas for 21 years and tried over 100 jury trials. During this time, he was appointed by President Ronald Reagan as U.S. Attorney for the Western District of Arkansas. At the age of 31, he was the youngest U.S. Attorney in the Nation.

Chairman BOEHLERT. Thank you very much, Mr. Secretary. Mr. Ford.

## STATEMENT OF MR. JESS T. FORD, DIRECTOR, INTERNATIONAL AFFAIRS AND TRADE, GENERAL ACCOUNTING OFFICE

Mr. FORD. Thank you, Mr. Chairman, Members of the Committee.

I am pleased to be here today to discuss the report which we are issuing to the Committee today on the need for improvements in the visa process to reduce the time it takes to adjudicate visas for science students and scholars. The State Department's Office of Consular Affairs, who adjudicate visa applications, must facilitate legitimate travel. At the same time, the United States has important national security interests in screening these individuals when they apply for a visa. Since September 11, visa operations have played an increasingly important role in assuring our country's national security. The State Department's goal is to adjudicate visas as quickly as possible, consistent with immigration laws and homeland security objectives.

Mr. Chairman, you asked us several months ago to conduct an analysis on how long it takes for a science student and scholar from another country to obtain a visa, and what factors contribute to the length of time in obtaining that visa, and also what measures are underway to improve the process. I will describe recommendations that are in our report that are designed to help reduce the time to adjudicate some types of visas.

It is difficult to estimate how long it takes to adjudicate visas for science students and scholars. According to the State Department, the Department has no set specific criteria or timeframes for how long a visa process should take, and data are not available on a number of visas that were issued or denied to science students or scholars, or how long the process took. However, a key factor that can contribute to the length of time for adjudicating visas is whether an application must undergo a headquarters interagency security check. This check is referred to as Visas Mantis. The check is required by the State Department, the Federal Bureau of Investigation and other interested Washington agencies when there are potential concerns that the visa applicant may engage in illegal transfer of sensitive technology, which could undermine U.S. national security. While state systems do not allow us to keep an aggregate—to keep aggregate data on security check processing times, State does have information on individual cases, which we use to conduct our own analysis.

We conducted a random sample of Visas Mantis cases involving science students and scholars that were sent from posts between April and June of 2003, and found that it took an average of 67 days for the security check to be processed. In September and October of this year—of last year, we visited seven posts, in China, Russia and India, and found the backlog of 410 cases outstanding for more than 60 days. We found that several factors make it difficult to resolve some of the security checks expeditiously. The process has several steps.

First, the post notifies the State Department and interested agencies that a security check is required. The agencies must conduct the check. The agencies have to notify the State Department of the results, and the State Department has to notify the post on what action to take. Because different agencies, bureaus, posts and field offices have different databases and systems, cases can get delayed or lost at different points in the process. For example, in fiscal year 2003, some cases did not always reach their intended recipient, and as a result, some of the security checks were delayed.

In some instances, posts' requests for security checks did not get to the FBI because the requests were improperly formatted. Also, inter-operability problems between the systems at the State Department and the FBI contributed to delays in processing time. The State Department and the FBI acknowledge that they have had problems in lengthy waits, and they—but they report that they have a number of measures underway, which they believe will improve the process and resolve outstanding cases. For example, officials from the State Department's Bureau of Consular Affairs and the FBI told us that they are working together to identify and resolve outstanding cases. Consular Affairs officials have told us that the State Department has invested about a million dollars to upgrade its technology for transmitting requests for security checks, and the system is expected to be functional later this year.

According to State, the new system will help reduce the time it takes to process security checks. State also indicated that our analysis of cases from earlier in 2003 did not reflect the current processing situation. The State Department has provided us with two samples that it has taken recently, which it believes shows that processing times are improving. These data do indicate that there is improvement in processing times, but they also show there are some continuing problems, and we were unable to scientifically validate either of the samples, so we can't—we don't know if they represent the entire situation.

Mr. Chairman, we are recommending that the Secretary of State, in coordination with the Secretary of Homeland Security and the Director of the FBI, develop and implement a plan to improve the Visas Mantis process to avoid unnecessary delays in issuing visas. In developing this plan, the agency should consider establishing milestones to reduce the current number of pending cases. They should develop some performance goals and measures for processing security checks, providing additional information to Consular Affairs that clarifies guidance on Visas Mantis program, and they should work to achieve inter-operable systems so that they can expedite the transmission of data between agencies. The State Department has indicated in their response to our report that they plan to study our recommendations and look for ways to improve the process.

Mr. Chairman, this concludes my prepared statement. I would be happy to answer any questions.

[The prepared statement of Mr. Ford follows:]

PREPARED STATEMENT OF JESS T. FORD

**Why GAO Did This Study**

Each year thousands of international science students and scholars apply for visas to enter the United States to participate in education and exchange programs. They offer our country diversity and intellectual knowledge and are an economic resource. At the same time, the United States has important national security interests in screening these individuals when they apply for a visa. At a House Committee on Science hearing in March 2003, witnesses raised concern about the length of time it takes for science students and scholars to obtain a visa and about losing top international students to other countries due to visa delays. GAO reviewed 1) how long it takes a science student or scholar from another country to obtain a visa and the factors contributing to the length of time, and 2) what measures are under way to improve the process and decrease the number of pending cases.

**What GAO Recommends**

GAO is making a recommendation to the Secretary of State, in coordination with the Director of the FBI and the Secretary of Homeland Security, to develop and implement a plan to improve the security check process known as Visas Mantis to avoid unnecessary delays in visa issuance. State commented it had taken some action to improve the Visas Mantis process and it would study our recommendation to make further improvements.

**BORDER SECURITY**

## Improvements Needed to Reduce Time Taken to Adjudicate Visas for Science Students and Scholars

### What GAO Found

State Department (State) cannot readily identify the time it takes for a science student or scholar to obtain a visa. State has not set specific criteria or time frames for how long the visa process should take, but its goal is to adjudicate visas as quickly as possible, consistent with immigration laws and homeland security objectives. GAO found that the time it takes to adjudicate a visa depends largely on whether an applicant must undergo an interagency security check known as Visas Mantis, which is designed to protect against sensitive technology transfers. Based on a random sample of Visas Mantis cases for science students and scholars sent from posts between April and June 2003, GAO found it took an average of 67 days for the security check to be processed and for State to notify the post. In addition, GAO's visits to posts in China, India, and Russia in September 2003 showed that many Visas Mantis cases had been pending 60 days or more. GAO also found that the way in which Visas Mantis information was disseminated at headquarters level made it difficult to resolve some of these cases expeditiously. Furthermore, consular staff at posts GAO visited said they were unsure whether they were contributing to lengthy waits because they lacked clear guidance on when to apply Visas Mantis checks and did not receive feedback on whether they were providing enough information in their Visas Mantis requests. Another factor that may affect the time taken to adjudicate visas for science students and scholars is the wait for an interview.

**Average Time Frames for Visas Mantis Adjudication Process, April to June 2003**

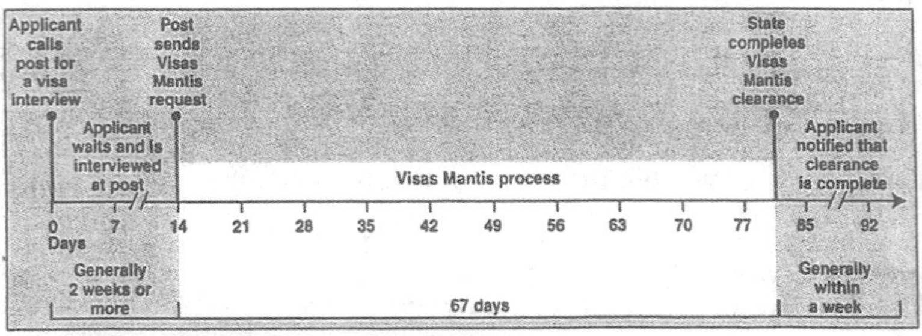


Source: GAO analysis of State Department documents and visa operations.

While State and Federal Bureau of Investigation (FBI) officials acknowledged there have been lengthy waits for visas, they report having measures under way that they believe will improve the process and that they are collaborating to identify and resolve outstanding Visas Mantis cases. In addition, State officials told GAO they have invested about $1 million to upgrade the technology for sending Visas Mantis requests. According to State officials, the new system will help to reduce the time it takes to process Visas Mantis cases.

Mr. Chairman and Members of the Committee:

I am pleased to be here to discuss the report we are issuing today on the need for improvements to the visa process to reduce the time it takes to adjudicate visas for science students and scholars.[1] Citizens of other countries seeking to enter the United States temporarily for study, exchanges, business, tourism, and other rea-

[1] U.S. General Accounting Office, *Border Security: Improvements Needed to Reduce Time Taken to Adjudicate Visas for Science Students and Scholars,* GAO–04–371 (Washington, D.C.: Feb. 25, 2004).

sons generally must apply for and obtain a U.S. travel document, called a non-immigrant visa, at U.S. embassies or consulates abroad before arriving at U.S. ports of entry. Since September 11, 2001, visa operations have played an increasingly important role in ensuring our country's national security. In deciding who should and should not receive a visa, consular officers must balance the need to facilitate legitimate travel with the need to protect the United States against persons whose entry could be harmful to U.S. national interests. For example, consular officers need to delicately balance U.S. national security interests with other interests such as promoting U.S. education and cultural exchanges, business, tourism, and the overall health of our economy. As part of the visa application process, many applicants with a science background, including students and scholars, must undergo an interagency security check, known as Visas Mantis, before being issued or denied a visa. A Visas Mantis check is required by the State Department (State), the Federal Bureau of Investigation (FBI), and other interested Washington agencies when there are potential concerns that the visa applicant may engage in the illegal transfer of sensitive technology, which could undermine U.S. national security.

At a hearing held by the House Committee on Science on March 26, 2003, witnesses raised concern about the length of time it takes for science students and scholars to obtain a visa and about losing top international students to other countries due to visa delays. You asked us to review 1) how long it takes a science student or scholar from another country to obtain a visa and the factors contributing to the length of time, and 2) what measures are under way to improve the process and decrease the number of pending cases.

**Summary**

State cannot readily identify the time it takes for a science student or scholar to obtain a visa.[2] According to State officials, the department has not set specific criteria or time frames for how long the visa process should take, but its goal is to adjudicate visas as quickly as possible, consistent with immigration laws and homeland security objectives. We found that a key factor that can contribute to the length of time for adjudicating visas is whether an applicant must undergo a Visas Mantis security check. While State's systems do not allow it to keep aggregate data on the number of Visas Mantis cases, State does have information on individual cases,[3] which we used to conduct our own analysis. We conducted a random sample of Visas Mantis cases for science students and scholars between April and June 2003 and found that it took an average of 67 days for the security check to be processed and for State to notify the post. Also, we visited posts in China, India, and Russia in September 2003 and found that many Visas Mantis cases had been pending 60 days or more. We also found several factors that made it difficult to expeditiously resolve some Visas Mantis cases. For example, in some instances, Visas Mantis cases sent by posts did not get to the FBI for its security check because of improperly formatted requests. Also, inter-operability problems among the systems that State and FBI use contribute to the time taken to process a Visas Mantis case. In addition, the consular staff at the posts we visited told us that they lacked clear guidance on when to apply Visas Mantis checks and did not receive feedback on whether they were providing enough information in their Visas Mantis requests. Finally, we found that the wait for an interview also may affect the time it takes to adjudicate visas for science students and scholars.

State and FBI officials acknowledge that there have been lengthy waits but report having measures under way that they believe will improve the process and resolve outstanding cases. For example, officials from State's Bureau of Consular Affairs and the FBI told us they are working together to identify and resolve outstanding Visas Mantis cases. These officials also told us that State has invested about $1 million to upgrade its technology for transmitting Visas Mantis requests, and the system is expected to be functional later this year. According to State officials, the new system will help to reduce the time it takes to process Visas Mantis checks.

State claims that the time taken to adjudicate visas for science students and scholars has decreased from last year. While this may be true, the data presented by State in support of its claim continues to show that some applicants still face lengthy waits. We acknowledge that there may be valid reasons for taking long peri-

---

[2] State data are not available on the number of visas that were issued or denied to science students and scholars or the length of time it takes to issue visas to these people. Consular Affair officials told us that State's systems can track aggregate student or scholar data by F (students) and J (exchange visitors) visa categories, but they cannot narrow their query search to specifically identify science students or scholars.

[3] During our review, State data were not available on the overall number of Visas Mantis cases or on the Visas Mantis cases by visa category. State's systems can track the visa process for individual Visas Mantis cases but do not allow for aggregate queries of Visas Mantis cases.

ods of time on some visa applications, given the national security concerns that may be involved. However, we believe it is important that State and the FBI continue to make improvements to avoid unnecessary delays. Therefore, our report recommends that the Secretary of State, in coordination with the Director of the FBI and the Secretary of Homeland Security, develop and implement a plan to improve the Visas Mantis process in order to avoid unnecessary delays in visa issuance. In developing this plan, State should consider actions to establish milestones to reduce the current number of pending Visas Mantis cases; develop performance goals and measurements for processing Visas Mantis checks; provide additional information to consular posts that clarifies guidance on the Visas Mantis program; and work to achieve inter-operable systems and expedite the transmittal of data between agencies.

Mr. Chairman, my statement today will elaborate further on the waits that may occur when Visas Mantis security checks are conducted and on the measures State and the FBI are implementing to improve the process.

**Background**

Visa applicants, including science students and scholars, generally begin the visa process by scheduling an interview at a consular post. On the day of the appointment, a consular officer reviews the application, interviews the applicant, and checks the applicant's name in the Consular Lookout and Support System (CLASS).[4] The consular officer then decides if the applicant will need a Security Advisory Opinion, which provides an opinion or clearance from Washington on whether to issue a visa to the applicant and may include a Visas Mantis check. In deciding if a Visas Mantis check is needed, the consular officer determines whether the applicant's background or proposed activity in the United States could involve exposure to technologies on the Technology Alert List, which lists science and technology-related fields where, if knowledge gained from work in these fields were used against the United States, it could be potentially harmful.[5]

After a consular officer decides that a Visas Mantis security check is necessary for an applicant, several steps are taken to resolve the process. The consular officer prepares a Visas Mantis cable, which contains information on the applicant, and then transmits the information to Washington for an interagency security check. The State Department's Bureau of Nonproliferation, the FBI, and other agencies review the information contained in the cable and then provide a response on the applicant to the Consular Affairs section of State headquarters.[6] The Bureau of Nonproliferation and other agencies are given 15 working days to respond to State with any objections. However, State has agreed to wait for a response from the FBI before proceeding with each Visas Mantis case.

Once State headquarters receives all the information pertaining to an applicant, Consular Affairs summarizes the information and transmits a response to the consular post. A consular official at post reviews the response and decides, based on the information from Washington, whether to issue the visa to the applicant.

**Security Check Is Major Contributing Factor to Length of Time It Takes to Adjudicate Visas**

State cannot readily identify the total length of time it takes for a science student or scholar to obtain a visa. However, in discussions with State officials, we learned that a key factor that contributes to the length of time is whether an applicant must undergo a Visas Mantis.

To obtain visa data on science students and scholars, and to determine how long the visa process takes, we reviewed all Visas Mantis cables received from posts between April and June 2003, which totaled approximately 5,000. Of these cases, 2,888 pertained to science students and scholars, of which approximately 58 percent were sent from China, about 20 percent from Russia, and less than two percent from India.

---

[4] CLASS is a State Department name check database that posts use to access critical information for visa adjudication. The system contains records provided by numerous agencies and includes information on persons with visa refusals, immigration violations, and security concerns.

[5] Under Section 212(a)(3)(A)(i)(II) of the Immigration and Nationality Act, an applicant is rendered inadmissible if there is reason to believe that the applicant is seeking to enter the United States to violate U.S. laws prohibiting the export of goods, technology, or sensitive information from the United States. 8 U.S.C. § 1182(a)(3)(A)(i)(II).

[6] The Visas Mantis program allows all participating agencies to provide information and raise any particular concerns that they may have regarding an applicant and/or the applicant's proposed activity in the United States. According to State, the key role of the Visas Mantis process is to protect U.S. national security, particularly in combating the proliferation of weapons of mass destruction, their delivery systems, and conventional weapons.

We drew a random sample of 71 cases from the 2,888 science student and scholar visa applications to measure the length of time taken at various points in the visa process. The sample of 71 cases is a probability sample, and results from the data in this sample project to the universe of the 2,888 science visa applications. We found that visas for science students and scholars took on average 67 days[7] from the date the Visas Mantis cable was submitted from post to the date State sent a response to the post.[8] This is slightly longer than two months per application, on average. In the sample, 67 of the visa applications completed processing and approval by December 3, 2003. In addition, three of the 67 completed applications had processing times in excess of 180 days. Four of the cases in our sample of 71 remained pending as of December 3, 2003. Of the four cases pending, three had been pending for more than 150 days and one for more than 240 days.[9]

In addition to our sample of 71 cases, State provided us with data on two samples it had taken of Visas Mantis case processing times. Data on the first sample included 40 visa cases taken from August to October 2003; data on the second sample included 50 Visas Mantis cases taken from November and December 2003. State indicated that both samples show improvements in processing times compared with earlier periods in 2003. However, based on the documentation of how these cases were selected, we were unable to determine whether these were scientifically valid samples and therefore we could not validate that processing times have improved. For the first sample, the data show that 58 percent of the cases were completed within 30 days; for the second sample, the data show that 52 percent were completed within this time frame. In addition, the data for both samples show that lengthy waits remain in some cases. For example, nine of the 40 cases had been outstanding for more than 60 days as of December 3, 2003, including three cases that had been pending for more than 120 days. Also, nine of the 50 cases were still pending as of February 13, 2004, including six that had been outstanding for more than 60 days. State officials commented that most of the outstanding cases from both samples were still being reviewed by the agencies.

During our fieldwork at posts in China, India, and Russia in September 2003, we also obtained data indicating that 410 Visas Mantis cases submitted in fiscal year 2003 were still outstanding more than 60 days at the end of the fiscal year.[10] In addition, we found numerous cases—involving 27 students and scholars from Shanghai—that were pending more than 120 days as of October 16, 2003.

**Several Factors Contribute to the Length of Time It Takes to Resolve Visas Mantis Cases**

We found that several factors, including inter-operability problems among the systems that State and FBI use, contribute to the time it takes to process a Visas Mantis case. Because many different agencies, bureaus, posts, and field offices are involved in processing Visas Mantis security checks, and each has different databases and systems, we found that Visas Mantis cases can get delayed or lost at different points in the process.[11] We found that in fiscal year 2003, some Visas Mantis cases did not always reach their intended recipient and as a result, some of the security checks were delayed. For example, we followed up with the FBI on 14 outstanding cases from some of the posts we visited in China in September 2003 to see if it had received and processed the cases. FBI officials provided information indicating that they had no record of receiving three of the cases, they had responded to State on eight cases, and they were still reviewing three cases. FBI officials stat-

---

[7] The 95 percent confidence interval for the average number of days to process a science visa application is between 50 and 84 days.

[8] According to State, factors that contribute to the length of time it takes to process a Visas Mantis check include investigations by clearing agencies or requests for additional applicant information. Once State sends a response regarding a Visas Mantis check, the post has to contact the applicant to issue or deny the visa. However, we did not attempt to determine how long this process takes.

[9] We assessed the reliability of the sample data provided by State by tracing a statistically random sample of data to source documents. We determined that the data were sufficiently reliable for the purposes of this report.

[10] Outstanding cases include those where the posts had not heard back from State headquarters and those where State had responded to the posts by indicating that additional information or review time was needed. The number of outstanding Visas Mantis cases is based only on F and J Visas Mantis cases for the posts in China but includes other visa categories for the remaining posts we visited.

[11] Posts have no way to ensure that State receives the Visas Mantis request, State has no systematic check to know if the FBI receives the cases, and the FBI has no way to ensure that its results are forwarded to the posts. Information regarding a case may potentially be sent back and forth between different agencies and offices several times before a decision can be made on whether to issue a visa.

ed that the most likely reason why they did not have a record of the three cases from State were due to cable formatting errors. State did not comment on the status of the 14 cases we provided to the FBI for review. However, a Consular Affairs official told us that in fall 2003, there were about 700 Visas Mantis cases sent from Beijing that did not reach the FBI for the security check. The official did not know how the cases got lost but told us that it took Consular Affairs about a month to identify this problem and provide the FBI with the cases. As a result, several hundred visa applications were delayed for another month.

Figure 1 illustrates some of the time-consuming factors in the Visas Mantis process for our sample of 71 cases. While the FBI received most of the cases from State within a day, seven cases took a month or more, most likely because they had been improperly formatted and thus were rejected by the FBI's system. In more than half of the cases, the FBI was able to complete the clearance process the same day, but some cases took more than 100 days. These cases may have taken longer because (1) the FBI had to investigate the case or request additional information from State; (2) the FBI had to locate files in field offices, because not all of its files are an electronic format; or (3) the case was a duplicate, which the FBI's name check system also rejects. In most of the cases, the FBI was able to send a response—which it generally does in batches of name checks, not by individual case—to State within a week. The FBI provides the results of name checks for Visas Mantis cases to State on computer compact disks (CDs), a step that could cause delays. In December 2003, a FBI official told us that these CDs were provided to State twice a week. However, in the past, the CDs were provided to State on a less frequent basis. In addition, it takes time for data to be entered in State's systems once State receives the information. In the majority of our sample cases, it took State two weeks or longer to inform a post that it could issue a visa. State officials were unable to explain why it took State this long to respond to post. Officials told us that the time frame could be due to a lack of resources at headquarters or because State was waiting for a response from agencies other than the FBI. However, the data show that only five of the 71 cases were pending information from agencies other than the FBI.

**Figure 1: Average Time Frames for Visas Mantis Cases, April to June 2003**

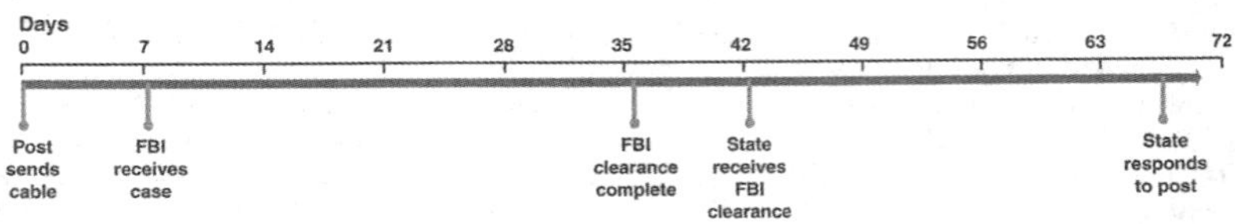


Note: Calculation of mean processing times and associated standards of error for sample of Visas Mantis cases, April to June 2003.

| Time interval | Average processing time in days | Standard error in days | Number of completed applications | Range of processing time in days |
|---|---|---|---|---|
| Post sends cable and FBI receives case | 7.9 | 2.3 | 71 | 1 to 82 |
| FBI clearance complete | 28.9 | 6.8 | 70 | 0 to 321 |
| State receives FBI clearance | 6.1 | 0.8 | 70 | 1 to 45 |
| State responds to post | 23.6 | 3.2 | 67 | 0 to 141 |

Source: GAO analysis of State Department documents and visa operations.

## Post Officials Seek Clearer Guidance and More Feedback

During our visits to posts in September 2003, officials told us they were unsure whether they were adding to the wait time because they did not have clear guidance on when to apply the Visas Mantis process and were not receiving feedback on the amount of information they provided in their Visas Mantis requests. According to the officials, additional information and feedback from Washington agencies regarding these issues could help expedite Visas Mantis cases. Consular officers told us that they would like the guidance to be simplified—for example, by expressing some scientific terms in more easily understood language. Several consular officers also told us they had only a limited understanding of the Visas Mantis process, including how long the process takes. They told us they would like to have better information on how long a Visas Mantis check is taking so that they can more accurately inform the applicant of the expected wait.

Consular officers at most of the posts we visited told us they would like more feedback from State on whether the Visas Mantis cases they are sending to Washington are appropriate, particularly whether they are sending too many or too few Visas

Mantis requests. They said they would like to know if including more information in the security check request would reduce the time to process an application in Washington. Moreover, consular officers indicated they would like additional information on some of the outstanding Visas Mantis cases, such as where the case is in the process. State confirmed that it has not always responded to posts' requests for feedback or information on outstanding cases.

**Wait for an Interview Can Also Add Significant Time**

Aside from the time it takes to process Visas Mantis checks, an applicant also has to wait for an interview. State does not have data or criteria for the length of time applicants at its overseas posts wait for an interview, but at the posts we visited in September 2003, we found that it generally took two to three weeks. Furthermore, post officials in Chennai, India, told us that the interview wait time was as long as 12 weeks during the summer of 2003 when the demand for visas was greater than the resources available at post to adjudicate a visa. Officials at some of the posts we visited indicated they did not have enough space and staffing resources to handle interview demands and the new visa requirement that went into effect on August 1, 2003. That requirement states that, with a few exceptions, all foreign individuals seeking to visit the United States need to be interviewed prior to receiving a visa. Factors such as the time of year an applicant applies for a visa, the appointment requirements, and the staffing situation at posts generally affect how long an applicant will have to wait for an interview.

**Agency Officials Cite Improvements**

State and FBI officials acknowledged that visa waits have been a problem but said they are implementing improvements to the process and working Improvements to decrease the number of pending Visas Mantis cases. For example,

- State and FBI officials told us that the validity of Visas Mantis checks for students and scholars has been extended to 12 months for applicants who are returning to a program or activity and will perform the same functions at the same facility or organization that was the basis for the original Visas Mantis check.
- FBI officials said that to address delays stemming from problems with lost case files or systems that are not inter-operable, the FBI is working on automating its files and setting up a common database between the field offices and headquarters. They also told us they have set up a tracking system within the FBI for all Security Advisory Opinions, including Visas Mantis cases.
- Consular Affairs officials told us that State has invested about $1 million on a new information management system that it said would reduce the time it takes to process Visas Mantis cases. They described the new system as a mechanism that would help strengthen the accountability of Visas Mantis clearance requests and responses, establish consistency in data collection, and improve data exchange between State and other agencies involved in the clearance process. In addition, officials said the system would allow them to improve overall visa statistical reporting capabilities and data integrity for Mantis cases. The new system will be paperless, which means that the current system of requesting Visas Mantis clearances by cable will be eliminated. State officials told us that the system is on schedule for release early this year and that the portion relating to Security Advisory Opinions will be operational sometime later this year. However, challenges remain. FBI officials told us that the name check component of the FBI's system would not immediately be inter-operable with State's new system but that they are actively working with State to seek solutions to this problem. Nonetheless, FBI and State have not determined how the information will be transmitted in the meantime. We were not able to assess the new system since it was not yet functioning at the time of our review.
- Officials from Consular Affairs and the FBI told us they are coordinating efforts to identify and resolve outstanding Visas Mantis cases. For example, they have been working together on a case-by-case basis to make sure that cases outstanding for several months to a year are completed. However, State officials said they do not have a target date for completion of all the outstanding cases, which they estimated at 1,000 in November 2003.
- In addition to improvements to the Visas Mantis process, State officials told us that they are monitoring post resource needs and adding staff as needed. These officials also told us that State added 66 new officers in 2003 and plans to add an additional 80 in 2004.

In conclusion, Mr. Chairman, agency officials recognize that the process for issuing a visa to a science student or scholar can be an important tool to control the transfer of sensitive technology that could put the United States at risk. They also acknowledge that if the process is lengthy, students and scholars with science backgrounds might decide not to come to the United States, and technological advancements that serve U.S. and global interests could be jeopardized. Our analysis of a sample of Visas Mantis cases from April to June 2003 show that some applicants faced lengthy waits. While the State Department and the FBI report improvements in Visas Mantis processing times, our analysis of data from the posts we visited in September 2003 and our contact with post officials in January 2004 show that there are still some instances of lengthy waits. State's and FBI's implementation of the Visas Mantis process still has gaps that are causing wait times for visas. State's new information management system could improve the Visas Mantis process. Nevertheless, it is unclear whether the new system will address all the current issues with the process.

To help improve the process and reduce the length of time it takes for a science student or scholar to obtain a visa, we are recommending that the Secretary of State, in coordination with the Director of the FBI and the Secretary of Homeland Security, develop and implement a plan to improve the Visas Mantis process. In developing this plan, the Secretary should consider actions to:

- establish milestones to reduce the current number of pending Visas Mantis cases;
- develop performance goals and measurements for processing Visas Mantis checks;
- provide additional information through training or other means to consular posts that clarifies guidance on the overall operation of the Visas Mantis program, when Mantis clearances are required, what information consular posts should submit to enable the clearance process to proceed as efficiently as possible, and how long the process takes; and
- work to achieve inter-operable systems and expedite transmittal of data between agencies.

In commenting on our draft report, State said it had taken some actions to improve the Visas Mantis process and it would study our recommendation to make further improvements.

Mr. Chairman, this concludes my prepared statement. I would be happy to answer any questions you or other Members of the Committee may have.

## BIOGRAPHY FOR JESS T. FORD

Mr. Ford joined GAO in 1973 and has worked extensively in the natural security and international affairs area concerning trade, foreign assistance, and foreign policy issues. He has managed GAO audits of the Agency of International Development, the State Department, and the Department of Defense.

In January 1994, Mr. Ford was selected into GAO's Senior Executive Service and, subsequently, was appointed Associate Director for National Security Analysis Issues. He subsequently, he served as an Associate Director for International Relations and Trade in GAO's National Security and International Affairs Division. In October 2000, he was appointed Director, International Affairs and Trade. He has directed the completion of numerous studies on U.S. natural security issues, foreign assistance, counter narcotics, and foreign affairs management activities and has testified before Congress on several occasions on these topics.

Mr. Ford received a Bachelor's degree in political science from Hiram College and a Master's degree in international relations from the Fletcher School of Law and Diplomacy. He is also a graduate of the National War College. Mr. Ford has received numerous awards throughout his GAO career, including the Meritorious Service Award and the Distinguished Service Award.

Chairman BOEHLERT. Thank you very much, Mr. Ford. Ms. Jacobs.

## STATEMENT OF MS. JANICE L. JACOBS, DEPUTY ASSISTANT SECRETARY, OFFICE OF CONSULAR AFFAIRS, DEPARTMENT OF STATE

Ms. JACOBS. Mr. Chairman, Members of the Committee, thank you for inviting me to testify on the visa process and its effect on the security of the United States, our economic, scientific and technological health, and our openness to other societies. Secretary Powell has succinctly articulated our policy as "Secure Borders, Open Doors," and we at the Department are acutely aware of the need to satisfy both of these objectives. Our universities reap the economic benefits of preeminence among destination countries for international students, and our scientific establishment flourishes in a climate of open exchange across borders.

While we are committed to facilitating the travel of legitimate visitors to the United States, we consider national security the highest priority in visa matters. The Department of State has long used specialized clearance procedures for the review of visa applications of individuals whose proposed activities in the United States may have security-related or other concerns. The purpose of the additional review is to focus on serious issues, such as hostile intelligence activity, potential terrorist threats, and access to sensitive technology.

One of the highest foreign policy and national security priorities of the United States is preventing the spread of nuclear, biological, chemical and other weapons of mass destruction, and their means of delivery. The Visas Mantis program, designed to address nonproliferation and technology transfer concerns, is an effective tool for U.S. intelligence and law enforcement agencies to support consular officers in screening individuals and entities that seek to gain controlled goods, technology and sensitive information in violation of U.S. export laws.

Under the current system, if a consular officer believes a particular applicant poses a potential threat under the Mantis rules, the post transmits a request for a security advisory opinion, or SAO, by cable simultaneously to the Department, the FBI and other interested agencies. The other clearing agencies generally take 15 working days to respond to SAOs unless they require additional time or information to clear a specific case. Consequently, the visa office may have a clearance from one agency, but may be waiting for another clearing agency to complete its review. The Bureau of Nonproliferation may also ask post to obtain more information from an applicant, which can take time and delay a response to post. Waiting for highly classified reports through appropriate channels can also delay a response to post.

The business, academic and scientific communities have all expressed concern that delays in Mantis procedures result in disruptions to ongoing research and commercial activities. We have taken steps to address these concerns by investing in people and technology, and pioneering new processes with our law enforcement colleagues that have solved many of the problems that we have encountered during the start-up period.

To increase efficiency, we have made a number of changes to staffing and procedures. We have created a stand-alone Mantis team that now has five full-time employees who are dedicated to processing only Mantis cases. We have procedures for expediting individual cases with the FBI. We were able to extend the validity of the Visas Mantis clearances, allowing for more freedom of travel to and from the United States, and we have put students and research scholars at the top of our appointment queue. We also periodically send the FBI spreadsheets of unresolved cases that are on hold, which they work through to provide us with a response.

The Visa Office, with input from the Bureau of Nonproliferation, will soon begin sending to the field a quarterly report that will provide feedback to posts on the quality of their Mantis SAO cables. The report will also include information from the NP Bureau on threat analysis and what technologies, groups or individuals might be of interest. The Bureau of Consular Affairs recently funded the travel of an officer from the Nonproliferation Bureau to attend a consular conference in China, the largest source country for Mantis cables. The officer met with consular officers from all China posts and discussed in detail the purpose of the Mantis program, what consular officers should be looking for, how to decide whether a case should be a Mantis or not, and what information to provide in the cable.

We are also using technology to enhance efficiency and provide for better statistical report. We have invested $1 million in the development of a cable-less system called the SAO Improvement Project or SAO IP, whereby SAOs will be made electronically through the Consular Consolidated Database. The new program will eliminate formatting problems. Beta tests of this program began last November, and we hope to bring all of our posts online during this year. The SAO IP will operate through the Open Source Information System or OSIS, which will provide inter-operable data transmission. Our partners are committed to electronic transmission of data over the OSIS network, and are taking complimentary steps to participate fully in the SAO Improvement Project.

The Department of State is working hand-in-hand with our colleagues at Homeland Security and the Justice Department to ensure that we have a system that properly identifies potential threats to the United States and stops them from reaching our shores. We also work every day with business and industry to see that access to our country is not impeded for those whose business we encourage and whose presence we value. We are determined to preserve the crucial benefits provided by these international visitors to the United States, as we work to strengthen the security of the visa process.

I am happy to answer any questions that you might have.

[The prepared statement of Ms. Jacobs follows:]

PREPARED STATEMENT OF JANICE L. JACOBS

Mr. Chairman, Members of the Committee:

Thank you for inviting me to testify before you today on the visa process and its affect on the security of the United States, our economic, scientific and technological health, and our openness to other societies. Secretary Powell has succinctly articulated our policy as “Secure Borders, Open Doors,” and we at the Department of State are acutely aware of the need to satisfy both of these objectives. The U.S. economy counts on the billions of dollars spent each year by international tourists, our universities reap the economic benefits of preeminence among destination countries for international students, our scientific establishment flourishes in a climate of open exchange across borders, and our entire society is accustomed to living in a free and open manner that counts upon an ease of movement across international borders. We are determined to preserve these crucial benefits to the United States even as we work to strengthen the security and integrity of the visa process.

While we are committed to facilitating the travel of legitimate visitors to the United States, we consider the protection of national security the highest priority in visa matters. The Department of State has long used specialized clearance procedures for the review of visa applications of individuals whose proposed activities in the U.S. may have security-related or other concerns. These procedures are carried out by the State Department at the request of and in coordination with other federal agencies. This is known as the security advisory opinion process. The purpose of the additional review is to focus on serious issues such as hostile intelligence activity, potential terrorist threats, and diversion of sensitive U.S. technology. A relatively small number of non-immigrant visa applications, less than three percent of our workload, are submitted by consular officers overseas to the Department of State for Washington-level screening by federal intelligence and law enforcement agencies.

One of the highest foreign policy and national security priorities of the United States is preventing the spread of nuclear, biological, and chemical weapons, their delivery systems and advanced conventional weapons. The Visas Mantis program, designed to address technology transfer and nonproliferation concerns, is an effective tool for U.S. government agencies to prevent entry into the U.S. of foreign nationals to gain controlled goods, technology and sensitive information in violation of U.S. export laws. Federal agencies review applications and provide the information needed by State to determine an applicant's visa eligibility under section 212(a)(3)(A)(i)(II) of the Immigration and Nationality Act. That section provides in relevant part that:

> Any alien who a consular officer or the [Secretary of Homeland Security] knows, or has reasonable ground to believe, seeks to enter the United States to engage solely, principally, or incidentally in—(i) any activity. . . (II) to violate or evade any law prohibiting the export from the United States of goods, technology, or sensitive information. . .is ineligible to receive a visa.

As part of their consular training at the National Foreign Affairs Training Center, all Foreign Service Officers assigned to consular positions receive 12–15 hours of training devoted to the processing of SAOs, including Mantis. During this training, the Non-Proliferation (NP) Bureau, which reviews Mantis cases in the Department, briefs on the proliferation threat and the importance of the Mantis screening process in helping to protect our national security.

The basic document that provides instructions to consular officers in the field on how to process Visas Mantis cases is the Technology Alert List (TAL). This is an annual cable that is disseminated to all posts at the beginning of every Fiscal Year. The cable contains two parts: the list of sensitive technologies and guidance to consular officers on how to process Mantis cases. The list contains some 200 technologies arranged in alphabetical order that nonproliferation and export control agencies have designated as sensitive for national security purposes. The TAL guidance cable describes the specific purpose of the Mantis program, instructs consular officers what to look for when reviewing an application that may result in a Mantis cable and provides details on what information to include in a cable. The guidance encourages consular officers to check with resources at post who might be able to help them decide whether or not a case should be submitted as a Mantis SAO. The cable further provides consular officers with a number of websites where they can access more in-depth information about the TAL technologies. Finally, the cable urges consular officers to use their judgment but to err on the side of caution when deciding whether or not Mantis considerations apply.

Under the current system, posts transmit Mantis SAOs by cable simultaneously to the Department, the FBI and interested agencies. We receive twice-weekly CDs from the FBI with updated clearance information on SAO cases. After the FBI name check unit runs the names of the subjects of SAOs through their name check system, they upload their responses onto a CD which the Visa Office picks up twice a week. The CD is an historical record of more than 500,000 responses the FBI has provided to us. The Visa Office uploads the information from the CD onto its own FBI Response database that it maintains as well as into the automated system known as VISTA, which is the Visa Office's tracking system for SAOs. Unfortunately, for various technological reasons, VISTA does not always capture all of the clearance information. If analysts do not find an updated response to a case in VISTA that they know is coming due, they must look at the FBI Response database to see if, in fact, FBI has cleared the case. In some cases it can take up to a week or longer between the time FBI responds to a clearance request and when the Visa Office analyst is able to send out the clearance response to post.

The other clearing agencies generally take 15 working days to respond to SAOs but, occasionally, they notify the Visa Office when they need additional time to clear a specific case. Consequently, the Visa Office may have a clearance from the FBI but may be waiting for another clearing agency to complete a review of a specific case. The NP Bureau may ask post to obtain more information from an applicant which can take time and delay a final response to post. At other times, the Visa Office must wait to receive a report from another clearing agency that may contain derogatory information pertaining to the applicant. Waiting for highly classified reports through appropriate channels can be another reason for delay in responding to post.

The business, academic, and scientific communities have expressed concern that delays in Mantis process result in disruptions to on-going research and commercial activities. A backlog did occur in the summer of 2002 when the Department mandated a positive response to all SAO requests. That requirement, combined with the sudden spike in additional clearance requests following the attacks of September 11, overburdened the system. Since then we have worked through many of these problems, invested in people and technology, and pioneered new processes with our law enforcement colleagues that have solved many of the problems of this start-up period.

To increase efficiency, we have made a number of changes to staffing and procedures. We created a stand-alone Mantis team that now has five full-time employees who are dedicated to processing only Mantis cases. We have procedures for expediting individual cases when appropriate. When an expedited clearance is needed, we fax such requests to the FBI, which routinely responds in a timely manner. We also periodically send the FBI spreadsheets of unresolved cases on "hold" which they work through to provide us with a response. The Visa Office, with NP input, will soon begin sending to the field a quarterly Mantis report to provide additional feedback. The Bureau of Consular Affairs recently funded the travel of an officer from the NP Bureau to attend a consular conference in China, the largest source country for Mantis cables. The officer met with consular officers from all China posts and discussed in detail the purpose of the Mantis program, what consular officers should look for, how to decide whether a case should be a Mantis or not, and what information to provide in the cable.

We are also using technology to enhance efficiency and provide for better statistical reporting. The Department of State has invested one million dollars in the development of a cable-less SAO process, called the SAO Improvement Project (SAO IP) whereby requests and responses will be made electronically through the Consular Consolidated Database (CCD). The new program will eliminate formatting problems. Beta tests of the NIV portion of the SAO IP started in Riyadh and Kuwait in November. (We started the beta test of the IV portion in Naples in December.) We began shipping the software for the new SAO NIV system to the field at the end of January and we hope to bring posts on line gradually as the year progresses. The State Department uses industry standards in designing our automated systems to facilitate data share with appropriate federal partners.

SAO IP will operate through the Open Source Information System (OSIS) which will provide inter-operable data transmission. The FBI is currently working on connectivity to OSIS in order to make full use of SAO IP. In the meantime, we are still sending case specific information to the FBI via cable. Once the FBI establishes connectivity to OSIS, they will receive all SAO requests electronically directly from post. The system will be much more efficient and will eliminate the human and technological errors that have occurred under the present system that relies on cable requests and responses. Our partners are committed to electronic transmission of data over the OASIS network and are taking complementary steps to participate fully in the SAO Improvement Project.

The Department of State is addressing other factors which affect visa processing times, including the biometric visa program and staffing levels. To comply with Section 303 of the Enhanced Border Security Act, the Department began deployment of the Biometric Visa Program on September 22, 2003, at the U.S. Embassy in Brussels, Belgium, and quickly followed suit at the U.S. Consulate General in Frankfurt and Embassies in San Salvador and Guatemala City. The program is now operational at more than 60 visa-adjudicating posts and with our aggressive roll-out schedule the program will be in effect at all visa-adjudicating posts by October 26 of this year.

This congressionally mandated program requires the physical presence of most applicants in order to enroll the biometric identifiers. To this end and to enhance security in the visa process, we established a new worldwide standard for visa interview policy. On August 1, 2003, new regulations were implemented which limit the waiver of personal appearance for non-immigrant visa applicants to only a few categories of exceptions, such as diplomats, children, and the elderly. This allowed all posts worldwide to ramp up their staffing in anticipation of the meeting the deadline. To meet additional staffing needs, the Department is establishing 168 new consular positions in FY 2004 and is requesting 123 additional positions for FY 2005.

We are working with the academic and scientific research communities to be as responsive as possible while maintaining the integrity of the process and meeting the goals of the nonproliferation program. Every spring as students begin applying for visas, we instruct all visa-adjudicating posts to make special arrangements to facilitate visa interviews for students and researchers. Some posts do not require appointments, some reserve appointment slots for students, and some assign specific days to student processing. Last October we obtained interagency agreement to extend the validity of the mantis clearance to one year provided that the applicant was attending the same program. Our Public Inquiries office treats all science-related visa inquiries as top priorities and has conducted extensive outreach efforts with the scientific and medical communities. We have also designated a Senior Visa Specialist as a point of contact for federal laboratories and other scientific establishments. Finally, we are establishing performance goals, whenever possible, of 15 working days from the date of receipt of the SAO by Washington agencies, after which the Visa Office sends a response to post as quickly as possible, provided clearances have been received from all clearing agencies.

The Department of State is working hand in hand with our colleagues at Homeland Security and the Justice Department to ensure that we have a visa system that properly identifies potential threats to the United States and stops them from reaching our shores. We also work every day with business and industry to see that access to our country is not impeded for those whose business we encourage and whose presence we value. We are determined to preserve the crucial benefits provided by these international visitors to the United States as we work to strengthen the security of the visa process. We want the world to know that we value our visitors and that we want them to come to the United States to enjoy the richness our country has to offer in so many areas. We want them and our own people to be safe while they are here and towards that end we are taking extra precautions, but America remains an open and welcoming country.

I am happy to answer any questions you may have.

Chairman BOEHLERT. Thank you very much, Ms. Jacobs. Mr. Garrity.

## STATEMENT OF MR. ROBERT J. GARRITY, JR., DEPUTY ASSISTANT DIRECTOR, RECORD/INFORMATION ADMINISTRATION, FEDERAL BUREAU OF INVESTIGATION

Mr. GARRITY. Thank you, Mr. Chairman, and thank you for inviting the FBI here to testify on this very sensitive question.

We appreciate the Committee's interest in this conflict between science and security in our visa policy. I have submitted a comprehensive statement for the record, but I will make a short statement, if you don't mind.

I would first like to say I hope that the GAO found the FBI both cooperative and forthcoming in developing their report. As this committee is very well aware, there is a delicate balance between allowing scientists and students into our country for education and exchange programs, and the necessity to protect the security of our homeland and our most sensitive technologies. As you have stated most eloquently, Mr. Chairman, it ain't easy balancing those competing interests.

The Visas Mantis program is designed to assist in the deliberative process by which we strive to recognize this balance. The Visas Mantis is a designation relevant to certain individuals who have access during their visit to American special technologies. The FBI provides specific name information to the Terrorist Screening Center regarding individuals about whom the FBI has a concern related to terrorism or other activities that could harm our national security. The Visas Mantis process is essential in looking at visa applications regarding those about whom we may have records, but about whom we have not gathered sufficient information to cause their addition to a watch list. We must protect the homeland by preventing the issuance of a visa to an individual who may seek to gain access to information or technology in the United States that may cause our nation harm.

The FBI receives information on the applicants from the Department of State by a variety of means. Either by a computer disc, from a cable, from any Embassy or Consul around the world, or in special circumstances, we'll receive a facsimile and give that expedited processing. The requests are all entered into the FBI's National Name Check Program. This information is then searched against our Universal Indices. The names are searched in a multitude of combinations, switching the first, middle, last name, as well as combinations of first and last, first and middle, etc. It also searches different phonetic spellings and variations of the name, which is especially important considering that many names in our indices have been transliterated from a language other than English.

A common question that we are asked is how long does it take to complete a Visas Mantis name check. As shown on the graph with my prepared statement, 88 percent of our requests are completed in 30 days, and 98 percent of the requests are resolved in 120 days. Most name check requests that are over 60 days old are the result of the time required to retrieve and review the field office record for information. One of the things that we have that is a concern to us is we have a decentralized record-keeping system. The FBI stores records in 265 locations worldwide. That is one of the issues that we are addressing, but we have to track down many times the file and find the information, wherever it may be.

I do want to emphasize to you that the FBI is sensitive to the impact the delays, and visa processing of students and scholars, may have on business, education, foreign relations and the worldwide perceptions of the United States. With these considerations in mind, the FBI is working diligently with the State Department toward the common goal of improving the expediency and efficiency of the visa clearance process. But at the same time, the consequences of our mission on homeland security requires that our name check process be primarily focused on accurate and thorough results. This does mean that there are instances when the FBI's review of a visa request must require as much time as needed to obtain an unequivocally correct result.

We are working together with the State Department to ensure that all old visa requests are accounted for and processed. This has been accomplished through a systematic comparison between the FBI name checks and the State Department's visa databases. We closely monitored student visa submissions for this school year, and believe that we were able to meet the seasonal demand. We are using the National Academy of Sciences' data to assist us in monitoring our response time for both students and visiting scholars. We have a public inquiry system where we check the status of individual cases, and this system has been helpful in identifying and resolving individual problems. We have not detected any systematic problems associated with our review process.

The FBI recognizes that the increase in numbers of requests necessitates the development of even more efficient processes in order to sustain the current pace of processing name check requests. We are in the process of implementing a number of interim improvements to minimize manual submissions by all agencies and to increase efficiency within our process. In addition, we have developed a high-level functional requirement for an entirely new name check application that would be compatible with these improvements. The new name check application is now undergoing review as part of our ITIM Process.

Additionally, the FBI is participating in the development of the Department of State's new visa database. As the existing FBI Name Check System is a legacy system that serves numerous other agencies, the data from the new Department of State database must be translated before it can enter into the FBI's Name Check System. This is not an insurmountable obstacle, however. Current planning is focused on the optimum method to move requests from the State Department to the FBI. In the interim, the State Department submits requests to the FBI from its new database by computer disk, and this process has proven to be highly reliable.

In conclusion, the FBI recognizes the importance of accurate and timely name check processing. I want to emphasize to you that this has the full attention of Director Mueller. We appreciate the Committee's interest, and I am prepared to answer any questions.

[The prepared statement of Mr. Garrity follows:]

PREPARED STATEMENT OF ROBERT J. GARRITY, JR.

Mr. Chairman and Members of the Committee, thank you for inviting Assistant Director Hooton here today to testify in this hearing, in which the Committee is reviewing the conflict between science and security in visa policy. Unfortunately, Mr. Hooton could not be here today, so I have been designated to provide testimony in his stead. My name is Robert Garrity, and I have served as an FBI Special Agent since 1976. I currently serve as the Deputy Assistant Director of one of the FBI's newest divisions, the Records Management Division (RMD). My goal today is to discuss the FBI's role in vetting foreign visa applicants under the Visas Mantis program. First, I would like to say that the FBI appreciates the Committee's interest in this subject and hopes that the General Accounting Office (GAO) found us both cooperative and forthcoming in developing their report on *Improvements Needed to Reduce Time Taken to Adjudicate Visas for Science Students and Scholars.*

**FBI Name Check Process**

The FBI receives information on the applicants from the Department of State via computer disc, cable, or manual (facsimile) submissions. The requests are entered into the FBI's National Name Check Program (NNCP). The information is searched against the FBI Universal Indices (UNI). The searches seek all instances of the individual's name and approximate date of birth, whether a main file name or reference. By way of explanation, a main file name is that of an individual who is the subject of an FBI investigation, whereas a reference is someone whose name appears in an FBI investigation. References may be associates, witnesses, co-conspirators, or victims whose names have been indexed for later retrieval. The names are searched in a multitude of combinations, switching the order of first, last, middle names, as well as combinations with just the first and last, first and middle, etc. It also searches different phonetic spelling variations of the names, especially important considering that many names in our indices have been transliterated from a language other than English.

If there is a match with a name in a FBI record, it is designated as a "Hit," meaning that the system has stopped on a possible match with the name being checked, but now a human being must review the file or index entry to further refine the names "Hit" upon. If the search develops a name and birth date match, it is designated an "Ident." An "Ident" is usually easier to resolve.

Approximately 85 percent of name checks are electronically returned to the Department of State as having "No Record" within 72 hours. A "No Record" indicates that the FBI's Central Records System contains no identifiable information regarding this individual. By agreement with the Department of State, partially due to our concern about the time factors in approving visa requests, a "No Record" equates to a "No Objection" to the issuance of a visa. The investigative divisions in the FBI, (i.e., the Counterterrorism Division, the Counterintelligence Division, the Criminal Investigative Division, and the Cyber Division) do not review visa requests where there is no record of the individual. Duplicate submissions (i.e., identically spelled names with identical dates of birth submitted within the last 120 days) are not checked and the duplicate findings are returned to State.

With the remaining 15 percent that were not immediately eliminated as a "No Record," because a name and birth date are not sufficient to positively correlate the file with an individual, additional review is required. A secondary manual name search usually identifies an additional 10 percent of the requests as also not being identical to an individual in our files, for a 95 percent overall "No Record" response rate. This is usually accomplished within a week of the request. The remaining five percent are identified as possibly being the subject of an FBI record. The FBI record must now be retrieved and reviewed. If the records were electronically uploaded into the FBI Automated Case Support (ACS) electronic record-keeping system, it can be viewed quickly. If not, the relevant information must be retrieved from the existing paper record. Review of this information will determine whether the information is identified with the subject of the request. If not, the request is closed as a "No Record."

The information in the file is reviewed for possible derogatory information. Less than one percent of the requests are identified with an individual with information that is derogatory or poses concern to the FBI about having access to sensitive or special U.S. technologies. These requests are forwarded to the appropriate FBI investigative division for further analysis. If the investigative division determines there is no objection to the visa request, the request is returned to the name check dissemination desk for forwarding to the Department of State. Results of the name check process are returned to the Department of State twice weekly by computer disc or telephonically in expedited requests.

If there is an objection to the visa request, the investigative division will prepare a written Security Advisory Opinion and forward it separately to the Department of State. In instances where the investigative division determines it appropriate, that individual will be placed on a watch list. In reviewing these visa requests, the FBI has, in the past, identified individuals attempting to enter the United States who are of serious concern to the FBI.

I want to emphasize to you that the FBI is sensitive to the impact that delays in visa processing of students and scholars may have on business, education, foreign relations, and worldwide perceptions of the United States. With these considerations in mind, the FBI is working diligently with the Department of State toward the common goal of improving the expediency and efficiency of the visa clearance process. At the same time, the consequences of the FBI's mission on homeland security requires that our name check process be primarily focused on accurate and thorough results. This means that there are instances when the FBI's review of a visa request must require as much time as needed to obtain an unequivocally correct result.

**Processing Times**

The FBI's goal is to have all visa requests completed within 120 days. Attachment A illustrates the current status of how long it takes to complete Visas Mantis name checks. This status is current as of February 23, 2004. For Visas Mantis, the FBI received 1,522 requests in the month of January 2004 and by February 23 had resolved 1,334, or 88 percent of them. In the month of December 2003, the FBI received 1,446 Visas Mantis requests and by February 23 had resolved all but 130 of these requests for a 91 percent resolution rate. The percentages continue to rise over time, with 95 percent of Visas Mantis requests resolved within 90 days. Visas Mantis are particularly difficult to resolve due to the predominance of requests from China and the commonality of Asian names.

A common question we receive is, "How long does it take to complete a visa request name check?" As shown on the graph, 88 percent are completed in 30 days and 98 percent of the requests are resolved in 120 days. Most name check requests that are over 60 days old are the result of the time required to retrieve and review field office record information. Some delay occurs at substantive analysts' desks, but this is to be expected. These analysts are assigned to an investigative division and are primarily assigned to the analysis of intelligence reports from around the world in order to support on-going investigations, or to support the flow of intelligence to policy-makers. Despite these significant and voluminous responsibilities, these are the best professionals to review information in our records and to then make an informed decision on whether a requester of a visa represents a threat to our homeland, or is interested in illegally acquiring targeted U.S. special technology. You will understand, however, that with the press of other business, the reviews of visa requests do not always achieve the analysts' highest priority in their assigned work. I would add, in response to one of the questions posed in the invitation to testify before this committee, that the investigative divisions believe the information found in the Visas Mantis requests they review is of use in their other responsibilities.

**FBI Visa Tracking System**

The FBI's name check application accurately tracks each visa request within the our name check process. At any moment, we are able to electronically retrieve the status of an individual request, including where it is within the name check process, determine which requests have been pending for a certain period of time, identify the FBI files associated with an individual, ascertain the result of a name search, identify the type of visa request, and generate the data found in Attachment A. This tracking capability serves not only the 200,000 visa requests submitted each year, but also the other 6.1 million requests submitted by over 70 other federal, State, and local agencies.

**Process Improvement**

We are working together with the Department of State to ensure that all old visa requests are accounted for and processed. This is being accomplished through a systematic comparison between the FBI name checks and the Department of State's visa databases. We closely monitored student visa submissions for this school year and believe that we were able to meet this seasonal demand. We are using the National Academy of Sciences' data to assist us in monitoring our response time for both students and visiting scholars. We have a public inquiry system where we check the status of individual cases. This system has been helpful in identifying and resolving individual problems. We have not detected any systematic problems associated with our review process.

However, the FBI recognizes that the increase in numbers of requests necessitates the development of even more efficient processes in order to sustain the current pace of processing name check requests. We are in the process of implementing a number of interim improvements to minimize manual submissions by all agencies and increase efficiency within the name check process. In addition, the FBI has developed high-level functional requirements for a new name check application that would be compatible with these improvements. The new name check application is now undergoing review within the FBI's Information Technology Investment Management Process.

Additionally, the FBI is participating in the development of the Department of State's new visa database. As the existing FBI name check system is a legacy system that serves numerous other agencies, the data from the new Department of State database must be translated before it can enter into the FBI's name check system. This is not an insurmountable obstacle. Current planning is focused on the optimum manner to move requests from the Department of State to the FBI. In the interim, the Department of State submits requests to the FBI from its new database by computer disc. This process is highly reliable and has improved processing times.

**Decentralized Recordkeeping System**

As I stated earlier, a significant factor in any delay in the FBI responding to a visa name check is retrieval of information from paper files. While many FBI files are available electronically, the majority of Visas Mantis checks pending over 60 days require review of physical, paper records currently stored at one of approximately 265 locations worldwide. FBI files are currently stored at FBI Headquarters, all 56 field offices, many of the larger of our 400 resident agencies, several warehouses around the country, in records centers operated either by the National Archives and Records Administration (NARA) or a commercial concern, four large Information Technology Center facilities on the east and west coast, and at Legal Attaché offices worldwide. Delays result from NNCP personnel identifying a file's location and then requesting the relevant information from a field office. Time delays mount as field office staff search file rooms and then fax or ship copies of the needed file or a prepared summary to FBI Headquarters. This process, repeated for many tasks, not only dilutes the FBI's responsiveness, but also limits information sharing, a critical success factor in protecting the security of our homeland and working counterintelligence and counterterrorism cases.

One possible solution to these problems the FBI is exploring is the establishment of a central records complex where all of our closed paper files would be located, and our active files stored electronically. Our frequently requested closed files could be scanned and uploaded into our electronic record-keeping system, so that Agents and analysts worldwide would have instant electronic access to the information they require for their jobs.

**Conclusion**

The FBI recognizes the importance of accurate and timely name check processing. I want to emphasize to you, this issue has the full attention of Director Mueller and Assistant Director Hooton. The FBI appreciates the interest of the Committee in this matter. To ensure the Committee's specific pre-testimonial questions have been answered, I have attached an addendum that discusses them directly. The FBI welcomes any further study by the GAO on this issue. I am prepared to answer any questions the Committee may have.

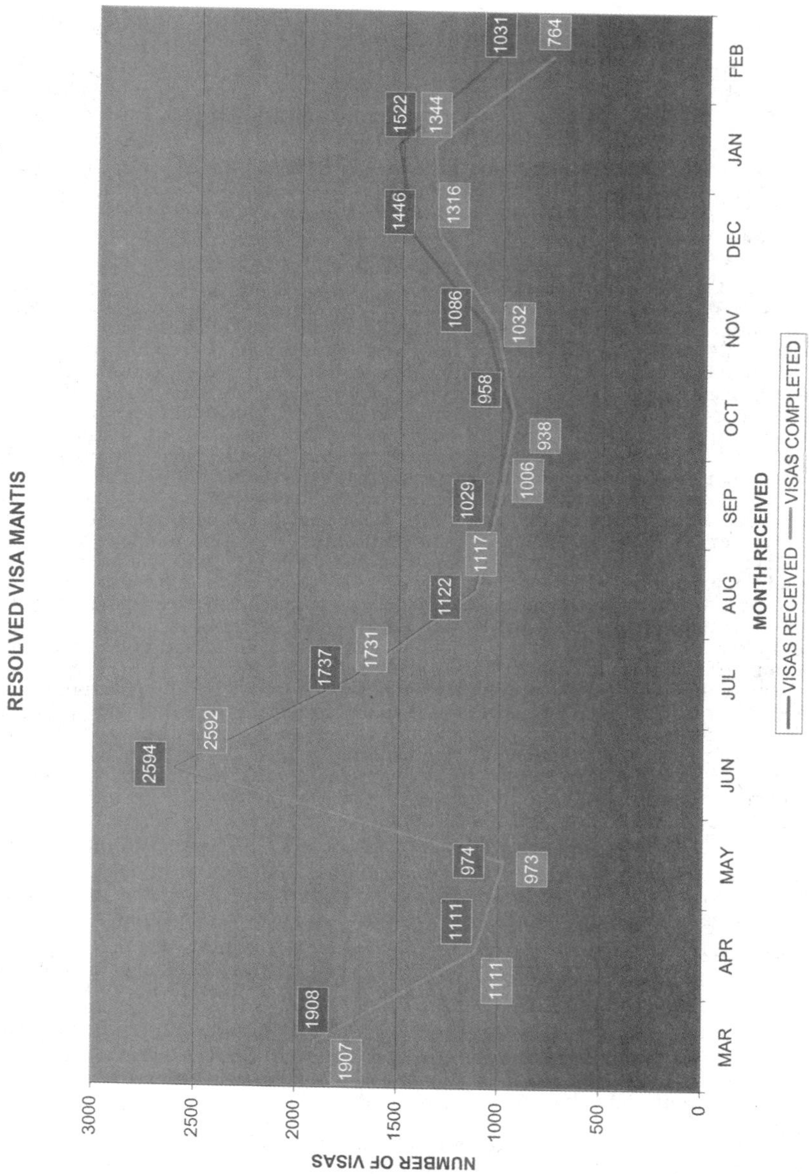
RESOLVED VISA MANTIS
NUMBER OF VISAS
0
500
1000
1500
2000
2500
3000
MONTH RECEIVED
MAR
APR
MAY
JUN
JUL
AUG
SEP
OCT
NOV
DEC
JAN
FEB
1908
1907
1111
1111
974
973
2594
2592
1737
1731
1122
1117
1029
1006
958
938
1086
1032
1446
1316
1522
1344
1031
764
VISAS RECEIVED
VISAS COMPLETED

**Questions submitted by the House Science Committee**

*Q1. How are Visas Mantis requests currently transmitted from the State Department to the FBI and from the FBI to the State Department?*

*A1.* The FBI receives Visas Mantis requests from the Department of State via computer disc, cable, or manual (facsimile) submissions. Results of the name check process are returned to the Department of State twice weekly by computer disc or telephonically in expedited requests.

*Q2. What is your internal process for tracking a Visas Mantis case? How often is that information available electronically? And how often must that file be located physically? What are your plans to fully automate this process? Have there been cases where a file has not been located and the applicant is still pending a response?*

*A2.* The FBI's name check application accurately tracks each visa request within the our name check process. At any moment, we are able to electronically determine the status of an individual request, including where it is within the name check process, determine which requests have been pending for a certain period of time, identify the FBI files associated with an individual, ascertain the result of a name search, identify the type of visa request, and generate a status report. We do not keep track of how often a paper file must be located, as opposed to having the information in our electronic recordkeeping system. As stated in my testimony, each name check entails every combination of the first, middle, and last name, which means that records may be found responsive for each combination. In addition, often there is a combination of paper and electronic files for each name. So, with one name check there may be numerous files, both paper and electronic, on a combination of name variations. As our system cannot quantify these numbers for us, it is too large a task to manually count and I cannot state how many name checks have required paper files. However, on February 23 there were 203 names that were pending over 60 days. It would be safe to assume most of these name checks required review of paper files. While we intend to fully exploit information technology, the system will never be fully automated. Files and information must be reviewed by human beings, which cannot be automated.

Now, if the question is more appropriately, when will it be fully electronic or the paper records digitized, the answer depends on our success in building a new central records complex and relocating all closed files to that location where the files of interest can be scanned-on-demand by an agent or analyst. There have been instances where files have not been located, but by agreement with the State Department, the FBI may close a case administratively if there are no counterintelligence or counterterrorism files associated with the name.

*Q3. What priority do Visas Mantis investigations have among other FBI work? How do you think these waits impact your ability, and the ability of other law enforcement agencies, to identify and capture a terrorist as opposed to simply preventing him or her from entering the country at that particular post?*

*A3.* Within the NNCP, they are a very high priority together with other homeland security name checks. As stated, the NNCP can resolve 99 percent of the name checks, with only one percent of the names and related files having to be reviewed by an investigative division. Within the investigative divisions, review of these files is usually assigned to intelligence analysts. These analysts are primarily assigned to the analysis of intelligence reports from around the world in order to support ongoing investigations, or to support the flow of intelligence to policy-makers. Despite these significant and voluminous responsibilities, these are the best professionals to review information in our records and to then make an informed decision on whether a requester of a visa represents a threat to our homeland, or is interested in illegally acquiring targeted U.S. special technology. Despite the press of other business, the reviews of Visas Mantis requests by the investigative divisions generally are handled expeditiously.

As for the impact of these waits on the ability to identify and capture a terrorist as opposed to simply preventing him or her from entering the country, I am not sure that can be quantified. However, I can say that the investigative divisions believe the information found in the Visas Mantis requests they review is of use in their other responsibilities.

*Q4. What steps are you taking to make [the] FBI's systems inter-operable with the State Department, which recently invested about $1 million to upgrade its technology for transmitting Visas Mantis requests? Until systems are inter-operable,* *how will information be transmitted and what impact will it have on processing time?*

*A4.* The FBI is participating in the development of the Department of State's new visa database. Current planning is focused on the optimum manner to move requests from the Department of State to the FBI. In the interim, the Department of State submits requests to the FBI from its new database by computer disc. This process is highly reliable and has improved processing times.

*Q5. How satisfied are you about the appropriateness of the cases referred for additional review under Mantis? Are consular officers providing agents with enough information and the right type of information in their requests?*

*A5.* The name check process culls out 99 percent of the Visas Mantis submissions prior to review by the investigative divisions. The information they review is useful and is focused appropriately on sensitive technology.

*Q6. What steps have you taken to improve the visa application vetting process? In light of the fact that there have been lengthy waits and there are still Mantis cases that have been pending more than 60 days, what measures do you have underway that will identify and resolve these cases?*

*A6.* We are in the process of implementing a number of interim improvements to minimize manual submissions by all agencies and increase efficiency within the name check process. The FBI has developed high-level functional requirements for a new name check application that will be compatible with the new FBI information systems in development. These new information systems, over time, will eliminate dependence on the retrieval of paper files. The development of this new name check application is now undergoing review within the FBI's Information Technology Investment Management Process.

## BIOGRAPHY FOR ROBERT J. GARRITY, JR.

Mr. Garrity was born and raised in the Baltimore, Maryland metropolitan area, where he received his early education. He graduated from the University of Maryland Baltimore County with a Bachelor's degree in psychology; the University of Baltimore School of Law; and earned a Master's of Public Administration degree from the University of Southern California. He entered on duty with the FBI in 1976 and, following a period of training, was assigned to the Savannah Field Office. In 1977, he was transferred to the Statesboro, Georgia Resident Agency. In 1978, he was transferred to the New York Office, where he was assigned to a foreign counterintelligence squad investigating the activities of the Soviet Military Intelligence (GRU). He was promoted, in 1980, to Supervisory Special Agent and transferred to the former Intelligence Division and assigned as an attorney to the Special Staff, the precursor to the National Security Law Unit. In 1983, he was reassigned to the Soviet Section, as a supervisor providing guidance, oversight and support to offices conducting counterintelligence activities against the former Soviet Committee for State Security (KGB).

In 1984, he was transferred back to the New York Office as the supervisor of a squad engaged in counterintelligence activities directed against the KGB. In 1989, he was promoted and transferred back to FBI Headquarters as the Chief of the GRU and Arms Control Treaties Unit in the Intelligence Division. In 1992, Mr. Garrity returned to criminal investigative assignments and was designated the Special Assistant to the Assistant Director, Criminal Investigative Division. In 1995, he was promoted to the position of Assistant Special Agent in Charge of the Dallas Field Office, where he was responsible for the day-to-day operations of the division.

In 2000, he was selected into the FBI's Senior Executive Service at the rank of Inspector, and assigned to the Office of Inspections. In this capacity, he was responsible for leading inspection teams to ensure field office and headquarters division compliance with existing policies and regulations, and to facilitate the improvement of performance by providing independent, evaluative audits of all investigative and administrative operations. He served as the Inspector-in-Charge of the Information Security (InfoSec) Working Group, analyzing the FBI's InfoSec policies, practices and procedures in light of the damage committed by a former Special Agent who was convicted of committing espionage.

In July 2001, Inspector Garrity was appointed the FBI's Interim Records Officer, reporting directly to the Acting Director, and charged with the responsibility of assessing the FBI's records management systems in light of the belated production of documents in the Oklahoma City bombing investigation. After assessing the records management system, Inspector Garrity recommended re-commissioning the Records

Management Division (RMD), to bring all records management functions under a central manager during the records life cycle. The FBI hired a professional records officer and then Inspector Garrity was detailed to serve as his deputy during the formulation stages of this new organizational entity. In January 2002, Inspector Garrity was detailed to the RMD as the Acting Deputy Assistant Director. On May 22, 2002, Director Mueller selected Inspector Garrity as the Deputy Assistant Director of the Records Management Division. From January, 2003 through January, 2004, DAD Garrity served as the Acting Assistant Director while the Assistant Director was on a special assignment.

## DISCUSSION

Chairman BOEHLERT. Thank you very much, Mr. Garrity, and you had some insight on a complexity of the issue, and I appreciate that.

Mr. Ford, I assume that you found all of the agencies, DHS, State and FBI cooperative?

Mr. FORD. Yes, we did.

Chairman BOEHLERT. Okay. Fine. So no problems in responding? And I would assume that all of the agencies are—did they have an advanced copy of your report?

Mr. FORD. They had an advanced copy of a draft of the report, which they commented on.

Chairman BOEHLERT. But I assume they are not just going to throw it on a shelf, but they are going to read it carefully and begin to study these things? Okay. Fine. Let the record show that all witnesses nodded yes in the affirmative. And I think we would all agree—let me see if you agree with this statement. That the current visa system operates in a way that oftentimes creates needless problems for foreign students and scholars, problems that don't enhance our security. Do you challenge that statement in any way? Mr. Hutchinson.

Mr. HUTCHINSON. Well, I just get a little nervous about conceding that point completely. I think there are certainly instances in which there has been needless delays or system problems in it. I think that the security regime that are—is in place is important and critical, but clearly, we have system problems to work on and there is work to be done to improve the process.

Chairman BOEHLERT. And let me applaud you and the Department for doing just that. I mean, you are moving in the right direction. I don't want anyone to think that this hearing is designed to criticize what you are doing. We just want to encourage you. We want to get some facts on the record, if you will, and go forward from here, because it is a changed world. I mean, just because someone in some distant point on the globe would like to come to the United States to study or to teach or to tour doesn't mean they can come here. I mean, we have an obligation to open our doors as much as possible, but our first obligation is for the security of the American people, and as I said in my opening statement, it just ain't easy.

Let me ask you this, Mr. Secretary. We all acknowledge there were some real glitches in getting SEVIS up and running, and I would assume you are in constant communication with the university community. And do your consultations with them, the dialogue, indicate that they feel that there is some substantial progress being made?

Mr. HUTCHINSON. Absolutely. We are first of all in regular contact with them. Jill Deary, our SEVIS program director, has weekly or regular conference calls with the associations representing the academic community, addressing problems on the SEVIS system or questions they might have. We are regular participants in their conferences. I personally have met with them rather frequently, listened to their concerns. But I think there were clearly some early glitches, and those have been addressed. From a technical standpoint, I believe they are satisfied with those, and I think it is illustrated by the fact that in the first SEVIS rule—interim rule that was put out, we had literally thousands of comments. The last time we put out a rule, there were 225 comments that came in.

Chairman BOEHLERT. So moving in the right direction?

Mr. HUTCHINSON. Absolutely.

Chairman BOEHLERT. Ms. Jacobs, one of the problems, it seems to me, is that a lot of consular officers around the world might be afraid to let someone in these days. They are going to err not only on the side of caution, but be doubly cautious. Is there specific guidance we can give to visa officers that would enable them to focus more on those most likely to present a threat? You indicated the China gathering, but the others I am concerned about. And secondly, to add to that, my experience and—appears over these years is that oftentimes, the consular officer in one of our posts around the world handling visas is a junior person, not a senior, more experienced person, because they go onto something else as they get seniority and experience. Let us talk about the consular officers, Ms. Jacobs.

Ms. JACOBS. Okay. Thank you for the question, because we consider the training of our officers to be a key component to this entire process. When new officers come in to the Foreign Service, they all go through basic consular training, and part of that training is devoted to how to do this security advisory opinion process. What the different checks are, what to look for. In addition to that, we send out every year a telegram that includes the technology alert list to all of our posts overseas, and the first part of that cable of course lists the various sensitive technologies. But the rest of the telegram is devoted to giving the officers guidance on what to look for, the types of technologies of concern. We tell them to consult within the Embassy if they have, for example, a science attaché to run the case by that person to see if, in fact, it does present concerns. We give them a list of websites that address many of the technologies in question so that they have more background on that.

Chairman BOEHLERT. Well—and my red light is on, but the same question, part two. I've learned this from Ms. Jackson Lee. Mr. Ford, is that your experience? When you are out in the field talking to the consular officers, do you feel that the guidance that they get gives them some comfort level in dealing with this issue?

Mr. FORD. Actually—well, you have to remember we were there in September prior to some of the things the State Department has recently implemented. But I can say that in particular in China and Russia, a number of consular officers there felt that they didn't have as much specific guidance as they would like in order to determine whether they were making the right decisions. For example, the technology alert list itself is a fairly extensive document. It has a lot of fields in it, and a lot of the consular officials were—that we met with indicated they had some difficulties trying to interpret, you know, how they were supposed to interpret that list and how they are supposed to apply it.

So they felt that getting a little more specific guidelines from the Department would have been very helpful, and if it sounds like the—I know the Department has told us they sent an individual to China, which of course is the key country in this issue. So hopefully, that issue has been improved, based on what we heard from last fall.

Chairman BOEHLERT. And just to follow up, Ms. Jacobs, the consular officer issue—am I correct in my general feeling that consular officers dealing with these issues are usually junior on the list, in terms of seniority and experience?

Ms. JACOBS. Yes, sir. In most of our posts, especially where we process large numbers of visas, the people on the line doing the visas are, for the most part, junior officers. But they are all supervised by more senior officers, and as I said, they do get training before they go to post. And let me just follow up just real quickly on what Mr. Ford said. We are giving them feedback on individual cases every day. We are in constant communication with Nonproliferation and the posts, passing information back and forth, and we hope with this new quarterly cable that we are going to send out, we are going to actually present samples of good cases and again try to reiterate what the officer should be looking for.

And in addition, we always talk about these SAO issues at conferences, consular conferences that we have. I have just recently been to three of these, and I spent a good couple of hours talking about all of these issues.

Chairman BOEHLERT. My time is up, but I just want to make sure you understand that we want to work with you because we don't want to deny our great educational institutions, the Cornells, the Syracuses, the Utica Colleges, a plug for my alma mater, to be denied the faculty and students the opportunity to contribute to those institutions. On the other hand, we are going to make darned sure that we don't let the wrong people in the country.

So it is very, very difficult, and every one of us up here have to understand it. And something else we have to understand. We are part of the problem. Mr. Garrity, I know about the whole system in the FBI, computers and everything else. I mean, talk about inter-operability and sometimes operating with yesterday's technology is a real problem for you guys. And you say we will solve the problem if you give us some money, so we have got to give some more resources dedicated to that so that you can talk to State and State can talk to Homeland Security, and you can do it instantly around the globe. So we will work on that too. Mr. Udall.

Mr. UDALL. Thank you, Mr. Chairman. I want to welcome the panel as well, and I want to direct my questions at Ms. Jacobs. Your visit here last year, you talked about IPASS, the Interagency Panel on Advanced Science and Security, and I understand in a recent communication with the Committee, the Office of Science and Technology Policy, OSTP, and the Department of Homeland Security have indicated they are putting together a plan to implement

IPASS. Can you talk a little bit about the current status of that and then what the schedule is, and I am going to turn to Secretary Hutchinson as well, when you are finished to comment.

Ms. JACOBS. Okay. Thank you for that question. The IPASS was an interagency group that we formed back in 2002 in order to get at the issue of advanced students coming here who might be studying in areas of sensitive technology. This group met and came up with a plan to try to complement the Visas Mantis program. They decided that they would look at technologies that are uniquely available in the United States. When Department of Homeland Security took over responsibility for IPASS, I understand that they are now looking at this and that they plan to set up a process within the appropriate time frame.

Perhaps Under Secretary Hutchinson can talk more about that, but certainly, the State Department has been a very active part. And as I said, the whole goal is to add value, not to add further delays to the processing system.

Mr. UDALL. So will it supplant the existing Visas Mantis system or add to it or compliment it? Is that still being worked out?

Ms. JACOBS. It is.

Mr. UDALL. Yeah.

Ms. JACOBS. I think the idea though is to complement it——

Mr. UDALL. Yes.

Ms. JACOBS [continuing]. To try to really target the interests on a certain category of students coming to study in areas of concern.

Mr. UDALL. I want to apologize to my colleague. It is actually Secretary Hutchinson, and he served here in the House. We are proud of what he is doing, so Asa, do you want to comment on the——

Mr. HUTCHINSON. Thank you, and former colleague is the best title I could have today, so it is good to be with you and I want to mirror what Ms. Jacobs indicated. We view IPASS as complimentary to Mantis, and I think we have to be careful that when IPASS was mandated, that was in 2002, before we had a fully compliant SEVIS system and before we had an implemented U.S. VISIT Program, both adding security measures for the entry of people into our country. But IPASS does have some specific application, particularly bringing on the academic scientific community to help us measure those that ought to have special review.

We want to make sure we don't do things that are duplicative and add an extra layer that would add to delays, so we are reviewing how IPASS can be utilized in a complimentary fashion, and that is an ongoing process that we have at the department.

Mr. UDALL. Secretary Hutchinson, have you—I am going a little bit off on a tangent here, but have you gotten any indication when you look overall at visa applications and—that the bad guys have tried to use this particular approach to get into our country to do mischief, or are we in a better be safe than sorry mode at this point?

Mr. HUTCHINSON. Well, first of all, it is clear that there has been instances of technology transfer. That some countries in the past have utilized our research, friendliness and academic institutions to gain knowledge and also the technical expertise, and so it is not just simply a terrorist issue, but also a technology transfer issue.

Mr. UDALL. Good point.

Mr. HUTCHINSON. And so I think the mandate is very appropriate that we look at these sensitive areas very carefully. But whenever you look at what terrorists are doing, they are looking at ways to avoid our visa system, where they do not have perhaps the interview process, where they don't have the background checks. And so the fact that these are in place have a deterrent value as well as a detection value.

Mr. UDALL. One of the messages you would want us to absorb is that this is as much about technology transfer concerns as it is about particular individuals using this particular channel in which to enter the country. That that is the greater challenge we face?

Mr. HUTCHINSON. Absolutely. That is correct.

Mr. UDALL. Yeah. I still have a little bit of time left, and I am going to hold off using the Chairman's technique until later in another hearing with the same question, part two. So I want to thank you all again for being here, and this has been very informative, and we look forward to working with you to find that balance that the Chairman so articulately mentioned and outlined. So thanks again.

Chairman BOEHLERT. Thank you very much, Mr. Udall. And without objection, I would like to insert in the record at this juncture a statement from the Association of American Universities dealing with this very important subject.

*[The information referred to appears in Appendix 2: Additional Material for the Record.]*

Chairman BOEHLERT. Mr. Smith.

Mr. SMITH OF TEXAS. Thank you, Mr. Chairman. First of all, let me make a couple of comments, and that is actually to compliment the folks who work for the Department of Homeland Security and the Offices of Consular Affairs and the FBI. They do a tremendous job with limited resources under oftentimes very stressful circumstances and conditions, so I just want to express my appreciation to you all and the people who work with you all for the jobs that you do.

In that regard, I want to read back again, Ms. Jacobs, a point that you made in your written testimony and also in your oral testimony a while ago, because I think it bears repeating. You said while we are committed to facilitating the travel of legitimate visitors to the United States, we consider the protection of national security the highest priority in visa matters. That was echoed by the Chairman a minute ago as well, but it is a point that ought not be forgotten in our—not haste, but in our eagerness to admit people who we want to come to the United States. That is really a second priority and comes after the need to protect America and American lives here.

Mr. Ford, in your GAO report, I just want to comment on your finding that—in regard to the Visas Mantis program, that it only took a little over two months to process those applications. To me, that is not burdensome, and in fact, as you all know, compared to most visa applications, that is pretty fast. In fact, two months is probably less than a lot of students wait to find out whether they have even been admitted to college. So when you put it in perspective, I don't think two months is too bad and all things considered, when you understand the importance of what we are trying to do to—that is to prevent would be or potential terrorists from entering the country, two months is, I don't think, unacceptable.

In that regard, let me direct sort of a two-part question toward Mr. Hutchinson and Ms. Jacobs, I think, and it is this. What criteria, other than what we are using under the Visas Mantis program, are you using or developing to enable us to differentiate between the prospect of terrorists and the legitimate student or scientist? And the second part is how does that criteria differ from what we used to use in the Immigration and Naturalization Service? Mr. Hutchinson, if I could ask you to respond first.

Mr. HUTCHINSON. All right. Well, first, you know, I would point out, according to my information, in China, the refusal rate for visa applications is close to 40 percent. Now that, in most instances, is not because there is a terrorist concern, but because there is a question as to whether they would return to their own country and whether they are, in fact, an intending immigrant. But whenever you look at the criteria we use, and of course, the consular office, in a direct application, is whether they are a legitimate traveler, and there are a number of measures that you look at in terms of whether they intend to return to their home country or not.

Secondly, from the terrorist standpoint, obviously we look at everyone who applies for a visa in terms of whether they are on a terrorist watch list, whether they have overstayed previous visas, which is an indication of risk, whether they have any criminal offenses. Those are all routine checks, and closer scrutiny is given to those that are applying for entry into sensitive areas, and that is where we have this more extensive review.

Mr. SMITH OF TEXAS. Thank you. Ms. Jacobs—and Mr. Hutchinson, I was going to come back in a minute and ask you how that differs from the INS, but I will do that on the second round. Ms. Jacobs.

Ms. JACOBS. The—well, as Secretary Hutchinson said, we continue to adjudicate visas in accordance with the immigration law. The section that Visas Mantis gets at is 212(a)(3), which talks about the illegal transfer of sensitive technology. As far as the criteria used, that sort of gets back to the guidance that we provide to the field. We give them a list of about 200 technologies that the interagency group back here has identified as being sensitive for national security purposes. And then we go further and try to explain what all of that means to the officers, what they should be looking for, what questions to ask. And as I said, we are doing additional training in that regard.

I think one of the biggest challenges that all of us face after 9/11 is I think we are doing a much better job of identifying bad people and getting those people into look-out systems. I think we have come a long way. We still face this issue though that we have to identify high-risk travelers who may not be known to us, who are not in a look-out system, and that is why we have these various screening processes in place, so that the case can come back for review to see if there are concerns that we need to be aware of.

Mr. SMITH OF TEXAS. Okay. That answered my question. Thank you all very much. Thank you, Mr. Chairman.

Chairman BOEHLERT. Thank you. Mr. Gordon.

Mr. GORDON. There is clearly a consensus here that this is, as has been said over and over, a both important and a sensitive issue, and that—you know, clearly that we should always err on the side of security. But that should also not be an excuse for inefficiency, and I think that is what we need to try to determine today. And Mr. Ford, thanks for a good report. GAO is—does a great service to Congress and the country, and this is once again, another good report. Let me ask you is this just—these delays, is this just a natural bubble in new programs getting started, and—or—and we have heard a variety—a list of things that these groups are doing. Do you feel like these are in order and feel like this is going to come together soon, or do you still see there might be problems?

Mr. FORD. Well, first of all, as we say in our report, there has been a lot of activity on the part of the State Department and the FBI in particular to address some of what I characterize as inefficiencies in the process. And I want to make it clear that GAO did not set a standard that 60 days is the—a right amount of time. Actually, if there is information out there indicating that somebody is going to do harm to the country, it should take as long as necessary. Our main point here is whether or not the process can be made more efficient, because we found cases when that didn't occur.

I believe that some of the steps that the Department of State and the FBI have underway can help improve the efficiency, particularly the transfer of information because when we started this project, clearly, there were cases when applications got lost. They were sitting on someone's desk. The process just had places where there could be gaps that good technology ought to be able to overcome. So if the Department's new data system works and if they can get it so that it is inter-operable with the FBI, a lot of the inefficiencies that we saw ought to be corrected.

Mr. GORDON. Well, we really need to have you back the 1st of next year and see how things are going. I think you are correct in that there shouldn't be—we could have a model time, but the time is whatever it takes. But again, that is not an excuse to let something just sit on a desk somewhere. Now the principle recommendation of GAO was that there be a coordinated plan between the various agencies, and my mother used to say that, you know, if it is not written down, you don't have a plan. So let me just ask Mr. Hutchinson—I know that you have responded—all of you have responded to this report and we are generally in agreement. But they didn't get into too much specifics.

Are you planning to work with these other agencies and have a written plan as to the Visas Mantis process, how to make it more efficient?

Mr. HUTCHINSON. Thank you, and I think there are a number of improvements that have to be looked at, based upon the GAO report. One of them of course is more State Department dependent, which is a cable-less SAO process, an online system that the FBI and the Department of State I know are looking to address. The second issue is——

Mr. GORDON. Mr. Hutchinson, I am not trying to cut you off, but my time is short here, and I am sure you are—really, the question that I have is do you intend to work with these agencies to develop a written plan to make it more efficient?

Mr. HUTCHINSON. We certainly intend to work with these agencies. In terms of a written plan, our responsibility at Homeland Security is to add the security perspective. If it takes a written plan to do that, we will certainly look at it. But we intend to address the issues raised by the GAO report from the Homeland Security perspective.

Mr. GORDON. Well, the principal—again, the principal recommendation was that there be a coordinated plan between the different groups. Ms. Jacobs, what about you? What are your plans in terms of developing a written plan for coordination?

Ms. JACOBS. One of the things that we are doing within State is to develop SOPs for handling these cases. For example, we are setting now a performance goal that if we can get all of the clearances back from the other agencies within 15 days that the cable will go back to the post within two to three business days. And so we are really taking a much deeper interest in looking at the processing times, at the numbers involved. This project that we have in place that will connect us with the FBI through the OSIS system will actually allow for electronic questions and answers to go back between posts and the FBI.

Mr. GORDON. Just—I know that my time is going to be running out. Again, I have no doubt whatsoever that each of your agencies are doing all that you can to try to make your agency effective and efficient, and I would just hope though that there needs to be a point somewhere where you have got to be talking together, in being sure that those things come together. And I would hope that you will, expect that you will, and look forward to Mr. Ford coming back next year with a hunky dory report.

Chairman BOEHLERT. Thank you very much. Mr. Smith.

Mr. SMITH OF MICHIGAN. Mr. Chairman, thank you. It seems to me this hearing should not be seen as a forum to pit the interests of science against the interests against security, but somehow work together to accomplish the same—the kind of compromise that is going to be good for our ultimate economy. Maybe the two goals are not jeopardizing our economic future and not jeopardizing the security of this country, and let me just ask you, Mr. Secretary, the question on the H–1B, 2 and 3s, are you increasing or decreasing—are you familiar with the increase or decrease in the green card, H–1B, 2 and 3s?

Mr. HUTCHINSON. Well, the—in terms of the green cards, of course, the President's initiative indicated that there should be a reasonable increase in the number of those. In terms of the B–1s, being a former Judiciary Committee Member, that is statutorily fixed as to the number of those, and I think that is something that will continue——

Mr. SMITH OF MICHIGAN. But of course, that is what we do here. We change that. It was much higher, now it is back down to 65,000. But a lot of students, as I contacted my universities, as Chair of the Research Subcommittee, a lot of the universities suggest that maybe even most of their students that are graduating with their doctorates in the science, math, engineering, etc., tend to stay in this country, and I assume they go from the restricted

F student visas and become more important and more educated scientifically, and then apply for an H–1B or a 2 or 3, and so I assume that is the——

Mr. HUTCHINSON. That is correct. That would be the process.

Mr. SMITH OF MICHIGAN. Just in terms of our future economy, we have worked very hard in this committee trying to encourage more interest and success in science and math with our students, and for a lot of companies that say look, lift—make it—relax the restrictions on the H–1Bs so we can keep our economy going, and after all, we have the prevailing wage provisions. I would just suggest that if demand increases, by increasing the salaries to available people in this country for their—those high-tech jobs, eventually in the long run, we are going to stimulate greater interest in the number of students and hopefully the number of parents that encourage their kids in K through 12. But it seems to me that as long as we already know that 9/11 had one person that was over here on a student visa, it is justified in getting tighter.

Have you—has anybody got any specific suggestions on how we facilitate that compromise to not jeopardize security, and I am also concerned about your restriction of visas for our scientific gatherings in this country. Already, some other country is saying look, come—for your international scientific forums, come to our country because it is too hard to get into the United States.

Mr. HUTCHINSON. We are in a transition, in my judgment. We have imposed new security requirements that are appropriate, from the interview of visa applicants to the biometric confirmation of identity. But it is important that we one, send the message that we welcome people to our country, and secondly that we are going to do everything that we can to facilitate that. That is the—we are going to have to improve our processes, our technology, and the message that we have to our foreign guests.

Mr. SMITH OF MICHIGAN. Anyway, part of the increase in demand is increased pay for some of these high-tech students in our country over the long run. I am introducing legislation that is going to be hopefully a stimulus and an awards system for those companies and industries that make a special effort to work with and improve our science and math in our schools in our country. But simply lifting the door to allow more immigration to replace our shortage by students coming in from other countries, I don't think in the long-term is the kind of solution that is going to motivate a better job in science and math education in this country.

Let me ask Mr. Garrity if we have become sophisticated in terms of the school reporting. Maybe I—in terms of the school monitoring what happens to these students, is that fairly—is that running smoothly and efficiently now?

Mr. GARRITY. I am probably not the best person to answer that question because they don't report to the FBI.

Mr. SMITH OF MICHIGAN. Who do they report to? Back to you, Asa.

Mr. HUTCHINSON. Yeah. The students coming in? It is——

Mr. SMITH OF MICHIGAN. No, no. The responsibility of schools to monitor what happens to these foreign students.

Mr. HUTCHINSON. It is really working very, very well. For example, the universities have a responsibility to go online, to tell us if a student is not complying with the visa, showing up for class, changing the majors inappropriately, these type of things. We have had 25,000 violations reported by the universities and academic institutions on SEVIS violators. Of those, only about 1000 were actionable leads that we could follow up on. But they are doing a good job cooperating with us and getting the information on student compliance with the visas.

Mr. SMITH OF MICHIGAN. Do you require personal interviews now for if there is an international forum in the United States from scientists from around the world? Do you require a personal interview? My understanding is, and their complaint is——

Mr. HUTCHINSON. That is correct.

Mr. SMITH OF MICHIGAN [continuing]. You now require a personal interview. Even if they come here twice a year or three times a year, shouldn't there be some kind of flexibility for a reoccurring U.S. visitor, whether it is business or whether it is scientific forums of some kind?

Mr. HUTCHINSON. Janice, do you want to take that? Ms. Jacobs might——

Ms. JACOBS. It is true that we interview the vast majority of people coming here for any type of visit. We changed that policy last year because we felt that we needed to be interviewing more people to really know more about the people who were coming here——

Mr. SMITH OF MICHIGAN. Well, my question is this. Somebody that comes once every year or every two years, there is no flexibility?

Ms. JACOBS. Well, a lot of that depends on the reciprocity schedule that we have with any given country. For example, if they are coming here to visit and they—in some countries, they can get a 10-year visa, which allows them to travel freely during that period. We wouldn't see them again for 10 years. If it is someone coming to a conference where there is sensitive technology involved, in that case, we might give the person a single-entry visa to come to that conference.

Mr. SMITH OF MICHIGAN. And sometime, it takes two months, I'm told. Thank you, Mr. Chairman.

Chairman BOEHLERT. Thank you, Mr. Smith. Dr. Gingrey.

Mr. GINGREY. Thank you, Mr. Chairman. I am going to direct my questions first to Secretary Hutchinson, and then to State, to Ms. Jacobs. First of all, let me just say that I was—during this recent President's Day recess, I went to Guatemala on a medical mission with the Flying Doctors of America. And we each were provided—those of us who speak no Spanish—with an interpreter, and my interpreter was a young Guatemalan lady who was in college in Guatemala. She actually would go to the university there on the weekends, and of course, work—had a full-time job.

In Guatemala, I think the currency—I think I am pronouncing this right, quetzales and eight quetzales equal $1. And they earn maybe the equivalent of 250 quetzales a week, and I was—the question I want to ask in regard to the fee—because I asked her why she didn't come to the United States and go to school, and she said because I don't have $100 to apply for a visa, and some of my friends or co-students have tried that and they pay their $100 and fill out the form, and a month later, they get a letter back telling them that they are denied. And that is the equivalent of about two weeks' wages, and, as you all know, many countries in Central America, and Guatemala in particular, are very poor countries.

So in regard to the amount that is charged, the question of course—and I will direct this to Secretary Hutchinson first. The former INS, which oversaw SEVIS before it was folded into the Department of Homeland Security in March, hired KPMG to evaluate whether a $95 fee they wanted to impose would cover the costs of the SEVIS program, and they actually came back and said it would more than cover the cost. In fact, a more appropriate cost would be $54. And for that reason, I think some may have been surprised when you proposed—your proposed rule included a $100 fee.

And so the question is what will the increased fee go to support that was not included in the original evaluation, and if you can address that problem. And, Mr. Secretary, before you do, this $100 fee or whatever the fee is, is if—if it is a standard, across-the-board fee applicable to students from any country, if the student is from Western Europe and an affluent country and, you know, with my—$100 may be nothing to them, but for this young student in Guatemala, it was impossible.

Mr. HUTCHINSON. Thank you, and certainly a very appropriate question. The fee is in place because Congress directed that this be a fee-supported program, and you are absolutely correct that the original study indicated that—I believe it was $56 would be sufficient for the administration of the program. But that was in terms of the administering the processing of the students, but it did not include the compliance side. And so we felt like it would be inappropriate to generate 25,000 leads and not have the ability to follow up on those leads. So the additional $44 is for the compliance side to follow up on the leads, to sort through these, and to make sure the students are complying with their obligations.

We are certainly sensitive to the burdens on the students and it is a fact and reality. We are sensitive to it. I know that many universities are trying to, you know, accommodate that burden on the students by giving them assistance.

Mr. GINGREY. And my second question—I know my time is getting short, and I will direct this to Ms. Jacobs. The State Department has almost no data that would enable policy-makers, including all of you, to know whether the visa system is focusing properly. And for example, we don't know how many cases are being referred for Mantis reviews or how often those reviews turn up a real problem. What are the Departments of Homeland Security and State going to do to make sure that we all have the data we need to evaluate the system, to see if it is truly working?

Ms. JACOBS. We do have some figures on the number of cases that we processed last year. We issued around 4.8 million visas, and out of those, we did about 220,000 checks, and that is all types of different clearances. In the case of Mantis, we did about 20,300 cases. And so I think in the big scheme of things, we can say that the percentage of people who have to undergo these additional checks is still relatively small compared to the numbers of visas that are issued.

Chairman BOEHLERT. Thank you very much——

Mr. GINGREY. Thank you——

Chairman BOEHLERT [continuing]. Dr. Gingrey.

Mr. GINGREY [continuing]. Mr. Chairman.

Chairman BOEHLERT. Mr. Weldon.

Mr. WELDON. Thank you, Mr. Chairman. I apologize for not being here for the whole hearing. I had an Armed Services hearing at the same time. But I do have some concerns here, and I am going to ask the Committee to support me in a request that I am going to make.

I have been working for the past 17 years on improving relations with a number of nations, both in the former Soviet States, Eastern Bloc, and now recently with North Korea and with Libya. In fact, we will take another delegation back to Libya this coming weekend, with the support of the Administration. The Chairman just got back from Libya. Was it last week? And——

Chairman BOEHLERT. Last week. Two hours in the deserts of Libya with Moammar Gadhafi.

Mr. WELDON. And we took a delegation over about a month ago, and so I am very familiar with the issue of visas, as it relates to our interaction with these nations that want to become closer to America. And while I, as a Member of the Armed Services Committee and Homeland Security Committee, understand the need for absolute security and absolute transparency, I will tell you that the process is broken. I can't tell you the number of times that our government has sponsored seminars with scientists and academicians, only to find that 24 hours before the event, 48 hours before the event, they can't get a visa to come in.

This sets our relations back with these nations years in terms of embarrassments. We have even had deputies from the Russian Duma denied. Now some of them legitimately have been denied because of questions about involvements that they are in, in the country. But some, there have been no reason given, and yet they have been denied access to the United States

So Mr. Chairman, what I would like to do, there—and I will—and I am also concerned about the system we have. We are working with Libya right now and there are very delicate discussions going on with the Libyans about a statement by the Prime Minister yesterday that appear to renege on the commitment relative to the responsibility of Libya on the Lockerbie crash and the bombing in Berlin. So I was on the phone all day yesterday afternoon with the—with my Libyan contacts right directly to the Prime Minister and the Foreign Minister, and with the person who is acting as intermediary who was given a letter by our Embassy, by our consular officer in Dubai last June basically stating—and I have a copy of the letter, which I will give you for the record—that your visa is approved from our standpoint. And this is the guy that is acting as intermediary who is helping us accomplish what we want to get the Libyans to reinstate the acceptance, which is going to happen today, which will allow us to remove the travel ban on Libya.

And so we have this letter from our Dubai consular office approving his visa and saying, but it is back in Washington being reviewed. When my staff called the State Department here in Washington this week, they said we have no record of this man. To us, he doesn't exist. He did apply at some point in time, for a visa in

Spain. Now my question is not whether or not this guy deserves a visa. My question is the left hand doesn't know what the right hand is doing if we have a letter from a consular office in Dubai, but the State Department back here doesn't even know the person exists. Now I don't know how you explain that and I don't know how we—and let alone figure out how we can increase the capability of getting legitimate people in this country and keeping out the bad guys.

I want to praise Asa Hutchinson, because it was the Homeland Security Agency this past summer, last summer, who prevented an ultimate disaster in having 20 young Russian high school students stay in America with 20 young American high school students, all of whom were nominated by Members of our Congress, the House and the Senate, and members of their Dumas, and they couldn't get visas to come over to spend time at the Freedoms Foundation for a conference on democracy building and free enterprise. It was only because of Homeland Security that we were able to get that issue resolved, and it was an embarrassment, but finally, it was rectified, and Director Hutchinson, I—Secretary Hutchinson, I congratulate you for your effort, and it was a very successful program.

So I am asking today, Mr. Chairman, and I would hope my good friend Bart Gordon would agree, that the GAO do an investigation, an independent investigation, and I would like to meet with them to give them some facts to work with, on the visa process relative to Eastern European nations and former Soviet States, specifically. And I would ask the Chairman and the Ranking Member if they would support that request.

Chairman BOEHLERT. Well, speaking for the Chair, I have—I would be fully supportive with the request, and Mr. Gordon has indicated the same.

Mr. WELDON. I thank the Chair, and I thank my colleagues.

Chairman BOEHLERT. Mr. Gordon.

Mr. GORDON. With students, I would assume that frequently the case is they are here for multiple years, and also for them to get clearance, you want to be sure that they are going to go back home, which means they have got family and things of that nature back home. So if you are going to be here for two, three or four years, you want to go home and see your family. Yet you have to go through this same—as I understand it, through the same process again. So I guess, Mr. Hutchinson and Ms. Jacobs, is it the case? You have to go through the same process, and if so, would there be a way to flag these folks and have an expedited process on their—you know, on a—they go home for three weeks to visit family on some holiday?

Mr. HUTCHINSON. Thank you, and actually the—if a student gets a four-year visa to go to the academic university, they do not have to reapply every year, and so that visa is good for all of their travel back and forth during that timeframe.

Mr. GORDON. That is not what we understand, but that is—I am—is that your understanding, Ms. Jacobs?

Ms. JACOBS. That is true for the students who are coming here who are not subject to the Visas Mantis process. We first of all look at their intention to return to the home country after the studies, and provided there is no other reason to find them ineligible for a visa; the vast majority of applicants would get the student visa to come here. I don't think——

Mr. GORDON. So what would be the difference between someone who was subject to the Mantis and someone who was not, and about what percent is that?

Ms. JACOBS. Well, it is a very small percent. Of all the checks we do, I said we did about 220,000 last year, only about 10 percent of those are Visas Mantis in general, and a smaller percentage of that would actually be students. But what we have done to address, I think your question is once they are cleared, if it is a student, for a particular program in the United States, we have worked with our fellow agencies to make the clearance valid now for one year. We are hoping to talk about getting that clearance to be valid for the entire length of the program, and that way, they can travel freely. They would not have to go through that check again.

Mr. GORDON. But it would seem like, by definition, if they have gone through this advanced check, then they have cleared, and so they ought to be in a different category.

Ms. JACOBS. No. We agree with that. The idea would be that they could come here for the length of the program. If there is somehow some derogatory information developed during the stay in the States, that would go into a look-out system to alert us.

Mr. GORDON. I guess my other question—you know, in the past, this was a vehicle for folks to come here and then just disappear and stay, and we wouldn't even keep up with them. And I know that you are doing a—you have got a tracking system now with this, I guess it is SEVIS? Is that how you pronounce it? But how much tracking is this? I mean, do—whether it is quarterly or by semesters? Are the universities checking in and saying yes, that this person did pass and that we know they are going to classes? I mean, how do you really keep up with someone a year or two later?

Mr. HUTCHINSON. The obligation on the university is to report any anomalies, and those can be specifically defined, but for example, if the student who comes in—first of all, they have to verify that they have been accepted before they would be entered, and then that they actually show up at class. And if they fail to show up at class or drop out, any anomaly—for example, if they come in to major in English and wind up having nuclear physics as their major, that is an anomaly that they should report online to our SEVIS program office.

Mr. GORDON. So they only report bad news. No good news? Just for——

Mr. HUTCHINSON. That is correct.

Mr. GORDON [continuing]. Terms of—yeah. Okay. Is this enough? Are you satisfied that—I mean, is this working and are the universities really doing that? Is there any spot-checking, you know?

Mr. HUTCHINSON. Yes. There is spot-checking. I am satisfied that they are very, very cooperative. Like I said, they have referred 25,000 anomalies to us.

Mr. GORDON. They have? Okay.

Mr. HUTCHINSON. Now some of those anomalies are misinformation or some confusion, and that is why the vast majority of those are not valid violations that we would pursue, but they are doing a good job of reporting. Now obviously, within that context, there would be a few schools that aren't, and it is a continued education and evaluation process.

Mr. GORDON. Ms. Jacobs, do you have any comments on that, or——

Ms. JACOBS. No. I agree with everything the Secretary said.

Mr. GORDON. Good. Thank you.

Chairman BOEHLERT. Thank you very much. In the report—and once again, my experience over the years has been that GAO reports are outstanding and they are well thought out. They have some specific recommendations that deserve to be addressed, rather than put on a shelf gathering dust. And I notice on page 24 and 25 of the report on "Recommendations for executive action," they say that "The Secretary of State, in cooperation with the DHS and the FBI should develop and implement a plan to improve the Visas Mantis process, and that plan should consider actions to establish milestones, to reduce their current number, develop performance goals and measurements for processing," and Mr. Gordon addressed that earlier, and we want to accommodate his grandmother, who likes to put things in writing.

You know, but you see what the recommendations are. They are very specific recommendations. Ms. Jacobs and the others, is this something you intend to follow, and might we get an indication of when we could hear from you, when this plan has been—these recommendations have been implemented?

Ms. JACOBS. Yes, sir. Thank you. We do intend to consider all of these recommendations very seriously. I think, in fact, we have taken some action on some of them. I mentioned earlier that we have established this performance goal now on the amount of time where we turn around a case. The inter-operable systems is absolutely key, I think, to increasing the efficiency of this whole system. This improvement project that I talked about, once it is up and running, should really go a long way to reducing delays.

Chairman BOEHLERT. Do we have in place the technology for the inter-operable systems to be up and running?

Ms. JACOBS. We are going to depend on the Open Information System, the OSIS system that was developed back in the mid-1990's to share the information from our visa database.

Chairman BOEHLERT. But when we could expect—give me a reasonable—and I don't say a precise hour and day and——

Ms. JACOBS. Right.

Chairman BOEHLERT [continuing]. Month, but when could we expect that we hear back from you that DHS, FBI, State all on the same wavelength, here is what they are doing in response to the recommendations contained in this GAO report?

Ms. JACOBS. Certainly, we talk to these agencies every single day about the process and ways to improve it. I think now we need to sit down together and develop a plan for putting all of this together so that we have a more——

Chairman BOEHLERT. Well, when do you think——

Ms. JACOBS [continuing]. Clear picture——

Chairman BOEHLERT [continuing]. It would be fair to call you back for a progress report?

Ms. JACOBS. I think maybe in six months.

Chairman BOEHLERT. I would like it a little bit shorter, but I will take that under consideration. We might call you sooner. Ms. Jacobs, let me—another thing. Although consular officers at some post told GAO that the most recent cable and using Technology Alert List was an improvement, many indicated it was still very confusing to apply, particularly for junior officers, and we know most of these are junior officers without a scientific background. To what extent are resources available to these junior officers to help them find answers to their questions about sensitive military and dual-use technology? And let me add, sad to report, we have a number of Embassies around the world without a science advisor.

Ms. JACOBS. Yes, sir. Well, where we do have a science attaché at an Embassy, of course, that is a very valuable resource for the consular officers to use. In our TAL cable, we also give them a number of websites that they can consult that give them more information about the particular technology involved. We don't expect them to be scientific experts, but we do, I think, give them a fair amount of guidance on what to look for, things to—and they can always come back and consult with us on an informal basis. But when in doubt, we do encourage them to submit the case for a review back here.

Chairman BOEHLERT. Let me ask you, Secretary Hutchinson, the same question I asked Ms. Jacobs. When can we invite you back to give us sort of a progress report on the implementation or the recommendations of GAO?

Mr. HUTCHINSON. Looking quickly at the recommendations, three of those are really more technical between Department of State and the FBI. They need to comment on their timeframes and capabilities. One of them though is referenced to training and guidance on policy, which is a Department of Homeland Security lead responsibility, and certainly, I think six months, we should have more information to provide in that regard. Policy changes take some interagency work do take some time, but we certainly do intend to start on it very expeditiously.

Chairman BOEHLERT. All right. Thank you very much. You know, in some respects, we are dealing with perception. We are—problems versus an inconvenience, and let me say what I—if I might amplify that. You know, prior to 9/11, I was typical of the American traveler. If I had a flight to catch, I would arrive about 10 minutes before, expect to dash up and say here is my ticket, get me aboard. And then prior to 9/11, when we have got these machines to process us through, I would stand in line and I would watch the people ahead of me be very upset with the screeners who were, at that time, making minimum wage with limited training. But screeners suggesting that they have to open up the purse or open up their bag, and they were very upset with that because they were being inconvenienced. Well, they—there was no desire to inconvenience anyone. There was a fervent desire to add to the security of everyone.

That has changed rather dramatically today, and sometimes, I find myself at airports where there is a rather lengthy line, and I don't find people complaining when the Transportation Security Administration makes them take off their shoes, for example, or remove their belt or something. So we are moving in the right direction, but in this instance, I still think there is a perception out there that we should instantly approve any visa application. It is a free and open society. It is not a free and open society anymore of necessity. I mean, we just can't do what we would like to do. And so if someone has to be slightly inconvenienced for a few more days of processing a visa or has to fill out yet one more form and—to enable all of your respective operations to review very thoroughly and to make a determination on security matters, so be it.

But I think you are getting the gist of our strong feeling up here that it is a changed world and there have been some problems and challenges presented, and I think you are addressing them in a responsible manner. We would encourage you to do so, to continue that effort, with as much dispatch as possible because foreign students at our universities, foreign faculty members at our universities, foreign distinguished visitors at our conferences all enrich America. They add something, and we don't want to stifle that. And I want to just address the old song that says where all of these foreign people coming into our universities are taking the place of American students and that is not fair, that is not the case at all.

Our experience is that students aren't being denied opportunities to go to school to study engineering or the various science disciplines. The problem is we don't have enough of them, and as Chairman Smith indicated, we have got to do a better job at K through 12 to prepare more students to go on to graduate training. And if we deny our universities students from beyond our borders, then what choice do they face? They have a lot of vacancies that we are not filling with American students. Then they cut back on the spending for their various departments, and the effectiveness is reduced, so this is a real big issue. And I think I want you to know how much we appreciate what each of you are doing to address this, working cooperatively with us. And once again, let me thank GAO for doing another outstanding job. And with that, I will turn to Ms. Lofgren for a final comment.

Ms. LOFGREN. Thank you, Mr. Chairman, and my apologies for being late.

I have been concerned for some time, as Mr. Hutchinson knows and the Committee knows, about the delays that students are encountering and the impact it is going to have on our ability to be an innovative technology society in the future. I mean, as we know, half of the Ph.D. candidates in the hard sciences and math and engineering are foreign students and, you know, that has been a huge engine of innovation for our country. I have a couple of questions about the use of technology as well as some systems that I think would assist.

I recently met with a group of primarily engineering students who were from various Middle East countries, and the interesting thing in talking to them—and these are very smart kids who were recruited by fine universities all over the world. I mean—and they didn't have to come to this particular prestigious university where I talked to them. They could have gone anywhere and were lucky that they came here. Because they were from Middle Eastern countries, they had special scrutiny, and they weren't even complaining about that. In fact, most of them hadn't been in their country of origin for many years. I mean, they had been undergraduates in America, and then they were in graduate school. I mean, they have probably been more time in America than they had been in the country they were from. They can't actually interview—in the case of Iranian students, they can't—there is no Embassy there, and so there was a problem in terms of doing the security checks.

A security check needed to be done in Iran, but they hadn't lived in Iran. They had nothing to do with Iran, and so they went to an adjacent country where they were trying to do an analysis, and in fact, the FBI analysis needed to be where they were living, in the United States. And these kids said—and they were great kids. Said we will tell you anything. I mean, come in, investigate us. We will take lie—whatever you want, because we want to be safe too from terrorists. But there was a real glitch in terms of just doing the analysis. And then the other problem they had was that once the analysis was done, it needed to be redone every time they needed to go out and come back in.

And I am just wondering is there a way to do the analysis once and to target the analysis where somebody actually lives and has the ability to—you know, where we can find something out, and then to give some kind of advanced reentry permit or something of that nature to students that we have thoroughly examined? Because what some of these students were saying is, you know, that if you are doing post-doctoral work, you need to go to these conferences in Europe and other places and then come back. If you can't go to the conferences, you really—it doesn't work, and you really can't be a post-doc at, you know, MIT or Stanford. You have to go to a European University instead.

What do you think—what—is that a possibility?

Mr. HUTCHINSON. I think that is the type of thing that should be examined, ways that we can help the frequent traveler that comes to conferences that has had a clearance. As Ms. Jacobs pointed out, on the Visas Mantis, which is the sensitive technology, the check is good for one year. And now, there is some rationale there. When you are dealing with sensitive technology, a check after one year is probably appropriate to make sure there is not additional information or they have complied fully with it. But if we can simplify that process and recheck—help that student out, then that is what we need to work toward doing.

Ms. LOFGREN. Now in terms of the inoperability between—I was, thinking, looking at you, Mr. Hutchinson, about a meeting that we went to. I think you were there and I was there. The Attorney General——

Mr. HUTCHINSON. Um-hum.

Ms. LOFGREN [continuing]. Asked us all, Members of the Judiciary Committee, to come and meet with him and have breakfast, and I—so we all did. It was a bipartisan group, and we spent the entire morning berating him and complaining about immigration functions, and now we get to complain to you.

Mr. HUTCHINSON. I have a totally different view these days.

Ms. LOFGREN. But—so I know that you, because you were complaining just like the rest of us, had the same level of frustration that we still have about inter-operability and the use of technology. And I am concerned that if we build our technology on what currently exists in the agency, we are building on a very fragile foundation, since it doesn't really work. I am wondering, are you looking at utilizing technology that might be more vigorous than some of the systems that have proved not to be robust?

Mr. HUTCHINSON. Yes. Absolutely, and one of the mandates that Congress gave us was to integrate the databases for our ports of entry. We have styled this mandate U.S. VISIT, and it has given us tremendous success in terms of making our systems a little bit more advanced, more capable, and certainly connected to the Department of State. But there is more progress that needs to be done. We need to upgrade many of those old legacy systems. You know, the—in the 2004 budget, the President asked for $400 million for that, and we got $330 million, and so there are some—and that will impact the ability to bring the systems up to date and to modernize those, but we will continue to work to do that.

Ms. LOFGREN. I see my time is up, but just one final question, and then maybe you can answer it subsequent to this. There is a fee increase being imposed. It is not for student visas, but in the whole immigration arena, and it is not clear to me how—I mean, I am not opposed to charging applicants the full cost for, you know, dealing with their application. But I am not seeing a clear trail of how the money has been used, and it is just—instead of getting quicker, it seems to be getting slower. I mean, you know, for not just students, but all types of applications, and I am wondering if you could provide, subsequent to this hearing, some——

Chairman BOEHLERT. Yeah, and——

Ms. LOFGREN [continuing]. Information on that.

Chairman BOEHLERT [continuing]. There—some other questions that we are going to ask that they respond to in a timely manner in writing. Earlier, Dr. Gingrey posed that same question, and he posed an intriguing thought. He was talking about a case in Guatemala where the income is, you know, dollars a day. They had—students there having to pay the same fee as someone in Western Europe where they make, you know, maybe a lot more than that. So we would appreciate a response in writing to that specific issue on the dollar amount charged and what the proposal is and how it is used.

Ms. LOFGREN. Thank you.

Chairman BOEHLERT. With that, Ms. Jackson Lee.

Ms. JACKSON LEE. Thank you very much, Mr. Chairman. Let me thank the panel for their presentation. Mr. Hutchinson, you realize that there is not a time when the Judiciary Committee is not in operation, and we are presently in a markup just a few floors down. I think you can remember that, so I thank the witnesses for their presentation, and I ask your indulgence, if I may raise some points that have already been raised. I am going to make a few statements, and then ask, as the Chairman has graciously allowed, that some of my questions be answered in writing because the Committee is still in the markup as we speak.

I think this is a very important hearing for any of us who live in university towns, and any large city, any rural area is impacted by universities and impacted clearly by the importance of their academic exchange, students on the undergraduate level, graduate students; all of them are a part of our vital energy and engine in this country. We realize that a page was turned on 9/11 and we must do a better job, but when I hear the numbers of the backlog that I think was noted by Mr. Ford, 67 days for processing and 410 backlog of cases in the region that he investigated, and out—more than—that are outstanding, more than 60 days. Obviously, we have somewhat of a problem.

So my question is how many actual man hours does the application process take? How much time is spent sending things back and forth? How much time is the application spending just sitting in an inbox, the pending application just sitting in an inbox, and how can we boost efficiency? Now I am going to want those questions to be answered in writing, and I would like to just get Mr. Hutchinson to answer this concern that I have.

I think that there is an inconsistency beyond the application process for our students as they are seeking visas to come into the United States or exchange for our professionals, our scientists, which I am delighted that the Chairman and the Ranking Member has held this hearing because these are important issues for the opportunities of our nation. But let me just point out to you that I think we also have a problem in enforcement of those entering this country in our respective airports.

There is an inconsistency, and I think it is partly training and it is partly I think the atmosphere that is suggested, meaning that we are getting terrorists. We are not getting terrorists if we are misreading their applications, the individuals coming in. We are interrogating people from Pakistan and India who are frightened to death and may say things that may be inconsistent and make them be perceived as a terrorist, and they are simply coming here, for example, to have—to testify in a lawsuit, accompanying their mother to testify in a lawsuit. It is a particular problem in Houston, Texas in that airport, which is in my Congressional District. The insensitivity of the questioning and the detaining of individuals who really have no interest, sense of purpose to do a terrorist act.

So to you, I am asking what kind of training is—are we providing those agents who are dealing with the individuals coming into this country with visas, by the way. Obviously, they could not come in with visas, who are randomly detaining people for no reason whatsoever and finding out that they have made mistakes, and have said oh, I apologize, only after Members of Congress have had to, in the wee hours of the night, intervene. So I think there is an inconsistency in training. We were discussing today the backlog in visas for the talented who may want to come over in exchange. But what is the agency doing about making sure that it refines its job to do what the American people want it to do? That is, to stop terrorism, but not to terrorize innocent visitors to this country, and that is what we are doing, and I would appreciate your response.

Mr. HUTCHINSON. Thank you, and obviously, sensitivity and respect is an important part of the inspectors' responsibility. We try to instill that in the inspectors' training and in their subsequent counseling. I think the vast majority of inspectors do a tremendous job out there, using good judgment and discretion. Obviously, there are individual cases in which bad judgment and discretion has been used, and we are happy to respond to any specific incidents or any case that you have and take a look at it.

But we do try to have that as an important part of the training and ongoing, and we do have a Civil Rights Officer that has been specifically statutorily designated for the Department that can review particular cases, where anything has been a problem.

Ms. JACKSON LEE. Let me thank you, and I might say that you do have a vast number of hardworking employees for the U.S. Homeland Security. I would invite you to visit Houston, as I have done before. I would like to have you come down and I would like to have you again visit our airport and again look at some of the operations. We are using U.S. VISIT. But I will look forward to the answers to my other question by writing, but I look forward to getting back with you, and I thank you very much. Thank you.

Chairman BOEHLERT. Thank you very much, Ms. Jackson Lee. And thank all of you, and notice the efficiency with which this committee operates. Secretary Hutchinson, we are going to meet your deadline of 11:30. For all of you, I know you have busy schedules and you have important responsibilities. We thank you for serving as resources to the Committee. This will not be your first visit on this subject to the Committee. We will extend an invitation to you in a timely manner for another visit. Thank you. This hearing is adjourned.

[Whereupon, at 11:20 a.m., the Committee was adjourned.]

# Appendix 1:

## ANSWERS TO POST-HEARING QUESTIONS

## ANSWERS TO POST-HEARING QUESTIONS

*Submitted to Asa Hutchinson, Under Secretary for Border and Transportation Security, Department of Homeland Security*

These questions were submitted to the witness, but were not responded to by the time of publication.

**Questions submitted by Chairman Sherwood Boehlert**

*Q1. GAO made a number of recommendations to reduce the time necessary to adjudicate visas for foreign students and scholars. Among them, GAO urged the Secretary of State, in consultation with the Secretary of Homeland Security and the Director of the Federal Bureau of Investigation, to develop and implement a plan to improve the visa process, with milestones for pending cases and performance goals and measurements for future cases. What steps are you taking to develop and implement a plan? Specifically, what are you doing to establish milestones and performance goals? How should Congress evaluate whether the planning recommendation is being implemented?*

*Q2. What work is being undertaken to achieve system inter-operability and to expedite data transmissions between agencies?*

*Q3. What would be an appropriate time for the Committee to have you back to review your agency's progress?*

*Q4. In the proposed SEVIS fee rule, foreign students will be required to pay their fee either electronically (with a credit card) or by a check drawn on a U.S. bank and payable in U.S. dollars. Are you concerned that the check option introduces a paper element into a system that was designed to be entirely electronic? How will you accommodate students from countries where access to credit cards and reliable mail systems is limited?*

*Q5. A foreign student already pays a $100 visa processing fee to the Department of State as well as a visa issuance fee determined by their country of origin—all before the applicant knows whether he or she will be allowed to enter the U.S. as a foreign student or scholar. Some have suggested a legislative fix to allow the SEVIS fee to be paid subsequent to the issuance of a visa. Would DHS support this statutory change? Why or why not?*

*Q6. Some have suggested that the Bureau of Customs and Border Protection (CBP), part of DHS, should collect the SEVIS fee at the applicant's point of entry into the U.S. This way, the agency benefiting from the fee is also the one responsible for collecting it. Does CBP have the capability to collect this fee? Assuming that Congress provides a legislative fix to allow the fee to be collected subsequent to the issuance of the visa, what do you think of having CBP collect this fee?*

**Questions submitted by Representative Bart Gordon**

*Q1. In your testimony you refer to the Visa Security Program, which has placed DHS personnel at consular posts in Saudi Arabia and which will be expanded to other posts. What is the role of the DHS personnel relative to that of the consular officers in reviewing visa applications?*

*Q2. Do the DHS personnel have scientific or technical knowledge, and do they advise consular offices relative to the need for Security Advisory Opinions?*

*Q3. You indicate in your testimony that, " DHS intends to review the Mantis process with the intent of incorporating the best elements of the IPASS concept without creating an additional layer of review." Are you working out how to develop this new approach for security reviews in consultation with the State Department and the Office of Science and Technology Policy?*

*Q4. What is the timeline for developing and implementing this new system?*

**Question submitted by Representative Sheila Jackson Lee**

*Q1. Please provide a timeline for a student visa application coming through your agency: who it comes from, what form it comes in (i.e., digital, or hardcopy, etc.), how you process it, what your role is (phone calls, letters of inquiry, compare to databases, etc.), how many actual man-hours are needed per application for those tasks (mean, range), how much time the application waits in a queue or inbox, and then where it goes from there.*

**Question submitted by Representative Lynn Woolsey**

*Q1. There have been cases at American universities, including incidents at the University of California campuses, where international scholars have had to be detained upon arrival in the United States because there were problems with their paperwork. Through some of the anecdotal information I have received, I have heard of professors and scholars, who arrive without having completed every step of a new clearance process, but they have letters from their universities, inviting them to the United States. In some of the instances, the scholars were harshly detained and poorly treated while their visa status was investigated. I am concerned that international students and scholars, whose contributions to American society and education are immeasurable, are afraid to come to the United States. They have heard horror stories about people being handcuffed, detained on wooden benches with a small blanket, and denied access to their luggage or medicines. Rather than potentially face this type of treatment, international students and scholars may choose to study or present their research in other countries. I do not have issue with the fact that their entry is delayed until problems are resolved, but I think there should be a protocol for handling these cases in a more reasonable and standardized way.*

*Do officials at American ports of entry have the proper training and financial resources needed to manage detained international scholars in a humane way that encourages them to come back?*

## Answers to Post-Hearing Questions

*Responses by Janice L. Jacobs, Assistant Secretary, Office of Consular Affairs, Department of State*

### Questions submitted by Chairman Sherwood Boehlert

*Q1. GAO made a number of recommendations to reduce the time necessary to adjudicate visas for foreign students and scholars. Among them, GAO urged the Secretary of State, in consultation with the Secretary of Homeland Security and the Director of the Federal Bureau of Investigation, to develop and implement a plan to improve the visa process, with milestones for pending cases and performance goals and measurements for future cases. What steps are you taking to develop and implement a plan? Specifically, what are you doing to establish milestones and performance goals? How should Congress evaluate whether the planning recommendation is being implemented?*

*A1.* The Department of State has prepared a plan to implement the GAO recommendations and is submitting it to DHS in accordance with the MOU with DHS concerning implementation of section 428 of the Homeland Security Act. Paragraph 4 of the MOU specifically addresses changes in the security advisory opinion process. We will inform the GAO when this plan has been finalized, and will continue to keep the GAO and Congress informed of progress. Meanwhile, we continue to make progress in streamlining the security advisory opinion process, which is a high priority. For example, we have created a new system for fully electronic communication of SAO data in near-real time, increasing both the speed and the accuracy of our communications. More than half of our visa-adjudicating posts are now using the new software for SAO data, and we are working with other agencies to establish fully electronic connectivity.

*Q2. It is my understanding that consular officers already collect fees from visa applicants to fund State Department operations. Some have suggested that consular officers should also collect the SEVIS fee. Do you support that idea? How might such a change impact existing fee collection processes?*

*A2.* The Department of State has no plans to collect the SEVIS fee, but we are working with the Department of Homeland Security to share our experience with overseas collection to determine how that model might be used to collect SEVIS fees. This is a fee of the Department of Homeland Security. We have thoroughly explained our thinking to DHS.

The Department of State has made many changes over the past few years to reduce the expense and burden of collecting visa fees. Our biggest collection effort concerns the non-immigrant visa application fee, also known as the MRV fee, from all persons applying for non-immigrant visas of any type, including student and exchange visitor visas. In many countries, we have instituted off-site MRV fee collection systems with local banks. In other words, the visa applicant appears at the bank to pay the fee and presents the consular officer a receipt at the time of the visa interview. This process minimizes the administrative burden on consular and financial sections of U.S. diplomatic offices in terms of personnel resources and safeguarding large amounts of cash. Posts overseas do not have the resources to collect the SEVIS fee.

We are concerned that if consular officers collect the SEVIS fee, or if the fee is collected as part of the application process foreign governments will see the SEVIS fee as an additional fee for student visas, and may increase the reciprocity fee for American students seeking visas in those countries accordingly.

### Questions submitted by Representative Bart Gordon

*Q1. GAO found that because the State Department does not maintain records on Visas Mantis cases by visa category, it was not possible to determine how many such cases involving students and scholars were being processed or the status of these cases at any time. What are your plans to begin tracking these cases? What are your plans with respect to establishing model timelines and benchmarks for cases subject to the Visas Mantis process?*

*A1.* The Department has developed the Security Advisory Opinion Improvement Project (SAO/IP) to improve the automation that supports the SAO process (Visas Mantis cases are one type of SAO). The enhanced software allows us to better track the progress of specific cases through the interagency clearance system. The software also allows tracking of cases by visa category. The software is in use in approximately half of our overseas consular sections. We expect to have all posts using the software by mid-May. At that point, the Visa Office will be able to monitor progress in all SAO cases through a variety of standardized reports.

Our suggestions for establishing timelines and benchmarks are being submitted to DHS. Per the MOU between the Department and DHS concerning the implementation of section 428 of the Homeland Security Act, DHS must concur in changes to policy and procedures involving SAOs.

*Q2. GAO indicates that the upgrades being carried out by the State Department in its information management system to allow for electronic transfer of data on visa security checks will not be immediately inter-operable with FBI information systems but that efforts are being made to provide inter-operability in the future. What is the status of upgrades to State's information management system and when do you expect to achieve inter-operability of information systems with the FBI?*

*A2.* To upgrade the automation that supports the interagency clearance process, visa processing posts overseas need new software. That software has now been provided to all our posts overseas. CA headquarters has verified that the software has been installed properly at 105 posts. We will continue over the next few weeks to verify with the remaining 106 posts that the software is functioning properly.

The improvement of connectivity to the FBI depends on our respective use of the inter-operable Open Source Information System (OSIS). CA is already using this network for other projects. We have no obstacles to expanding our use of this network. The FBI is now using this network with limited numbers of users. Once the FBI informs us that they are fully prepared to rely on the network, CA will transfer SAO data solely in an electronic manner. CA will then eliminate the transmission of such data in telegrams that have caused errors such as garbles in transmission to the detriment of efficient data processing.

*Q3. You indicate that State's Nonproliferation Bureau must sometimes ask consular posts for additional information about an applicant. Do you track the frequency of such information requests, and do you periodically inform consular posts on how to improve their security checks based on experience with past shortcomings?*

*A3.* The Nonproliferation Bureau (NP) requests additional information from consular posts in only about five percent of Visas Mantis cases. We work closely with NP to provide consular officers feedback on the type of information that is helpful for the screening process. In 2004, the State Department started sending a quarterly report to the field about Visas Mantis policy and procedural issues. The report also provides guidance that reflects current issues of concern to reviewing agencies. NP and the Visa Office (VO) give a training session on the Visas Mantis program to all consular officers before they head out to post.

The Bureau of Consular Affairs (CA) is funding trips by NP officials to regional consular conferences. An NP official attended a regional consular conference for China posts last January. VO also uses video conferences with posts that submit large numbers of Visas Mantis requests. For instance, we held such a conference with consular officers in Moscow in March.

CA is also creating a web page for classified information for use by consular officers. This will allow CA and NP to provide feedback of a classified nature to the benefit of consular officers around the world.

*Q4. The GAO study showed that the time required for State to transmit the results of an FBI clearance to a consular post was nearly 24 days, and could be as much as 141 days. What are some of the reasons for these very long delay times? What steps have you taken to reduce delays?*

*A4.* Upon receipt of a final response from all reviewing agencies, our goal is to transmit a response to post within two business days. Delays that occurred a year ago related to problems with telegraphic transmission, glitches in the data transferred between the FBI and the Visa Office, and shortcomings in the software in use in the Visa Office. To fix such problems, we developed new software and added personnel resources. We analyzed the results of the pilot program for the improved software to handle transmission of clearances and case tracking. We believe that we have successfully addressed the causes of the delays that GAO found. The new software is in place in approximately half of our overseas posts. We should complete this project over the next few months.

*Q5. What is the source of the technical problem you mentioned in your testimony regarding State's automated visa tracking system failing to capture all of the clearance information from FBI's security reviews?*

*A5.* The technical problem mentioned is due to a lack of a shared unique identifier in both, the Visa Office's internal case tracking system (VISTA), and the FBI response Database. VISTA uses the Post's cable transmission number, applicant name, and date of birth to identify a response record from the FBI. However, when the FBI response does not report this data accurately, VISTA cannot identify a matching record. The most significant problem with data received from the FBI is that the FBI reformats names that come into its name-check unit. Multiple last names are combined into one name.

For example, if a cable is sent with the name EL AHI, SEYED, the FBI will reformat it to ELAHI, SEYED. When the FBI sends its response back to VO, the record has the reformatted name and therefore VISTA will not be able to match the record. According to VISTA data, about 17 percent of all SAOs from FY 2003 had this problem. The Security Advisory Opinion Improvement Project (SAO/IP) eliminates this problem because it does establish a unique identifier for each transaction. The FBI concurs with this solution.

## Question submitted by Representative Sheila Jackson Lee

*Q1. Please provide a timeline for a student visa application coming through your agency: who it comes from, what form it comes in (i.e., digital, or hardcopy, etc.), how you process it, what your role is (phone calls, letters of inquiry, compare to databases, etc.), how many actual man-hours are needed per application for those tasks (mean, range), how much time the application waits in a queue or in-box, and then where it goes from there.*

*A1.* The majority of student visa applicants receive a decision concerning visa eligibility from the consular officer upon conclusion of the visa interview. Some cases may be suspended for anti-fraud work. Some cases that raise national security concerns may need to be submitted for interagency review in Washington. The interagency screening process is normally concluded within 30 days.

*Initial Steps*

An educational institution issues a Form I–20 to a prospective student and registers the student in the on-line Student and Exchange Visitor Information System ("SEVIS") maintained by the Department of Homeland Security (DHS).

Once the student has compiled all appropriate supporting documentation, the student may obtain an appointment for a visa interview at a U.S. Consulate. The minimum supporting documentation includes the visa application forms (DS 156, 157, and 158), a photo, a valid passport, and a receipt for payment of the visa application fee (also known as the MRV fee). Different consulates have different systems for making visa appointments, depending on local conditions.

Consulates worldwide give priority to student and exchange visitor applications. At this time, appointments are available around the world within a week except at five posts. The Department is helping those five posts with additional resources and/or management assistance.

The student may apply for a visa at any time before the initial program start date for his/her initial entry as a student to the United States. However, a visa may not be issued for an initial-entry until 90 days before the program start date.

*Visa Application at the Consulate*

When a student arrives at the consulate, s/he will normally turn in the application form so that clerical staff can undertake data entry. Visa applicants may now fill out their visa applications on line. The data is downloaded into a data base. At the consulate the student presents a print-out of the application with a bar code, and the information on the form is downloaded onto the visa processing system based on the bar code. Applications written manually are still accepted, and consulate staff transcribe the information on these applications into the consular database. Data entry may take a few minutes to approximately an hour.

The next step would be biometric collection. At over 100 posts, consular officers are now collecting biometric identifiers of all visa applicants. The biometric collection consists of a digital photo and an electronic scan of the applicant's two index fingerprints. All posts will be processing biovisas in accordance with section 303 of EBVERSA by October 26, 2004. This step occurs in front of the consular officer and takes approximately 30 seconds.

The consular officer will then normally take a minute or two to quickly look over the supporting documentation to determine the nature of the application and decide how to initiate the visa interview.

*Visa Adjudication*

The consular officer is responsible for conducting the visa interview. It is viewed as an important tool in determining the bona fide nature of a visa application. Immigration law places the burden of proof on the student to demonstrate that s/he is a bona fide non-immigrant who has the intention to return to his/her home country after a temporary stay in the United States, is a bona fide student able to pursue the proposed course of study, demonstrates funds for the proposed course of study, and is either proficient in English or will receive English language study in the United States. There is no fixed length for the interview; but the average interview of a bona fide applicant lasts about five minutes.

During the visa interview, the consular officer checks the SEVIS database to make sure that the I–20 is valid and that the student is still in active status within the system. If the consular officer approves the visa for issuance, that information is automatically sent to the SEVIS database.

*Name-checks*

When an applicant is entered into the consular database, a name-check is automatically done on the applicant's name in the Consular Lookout and Support System (CLASS). The consular officer has the results of that name-check at the interview, and verifies whether or not any "hits" pertain to the applicant. If there is a "hit" that appears to pertain to the visa applicant, the consular officer will deny the visa application under section 221 (g) of the Immigration and Nationality Act. This is a technical denial to indicate that further administrative processing is required. The consular officer will pursue the case with the agency that developed the derogatory information. In some instances, the Visa Office may act as intermediary. It normally takes 2–3 weeks for the consular officer to receive the appropriate background information and call in the applicant to discuss further a potential visa ineligibility.

In some instances, the consular officer will notice that an application raises national security concerns as identified by federal intelligence and law enforcement agencies. The criteria for cases that require screening through an interagency process are included in the Foreign Affairs Manual. The consular officer will deny the case under section 221 (g) pending guidance from Washington. The Visa Office acts as a clearinghouse, receiving and analyzing responses from the clearing agencies. The Visa Office provides final guidance to the consular officer. Most such cases are fully resolved within a month.

There are two types of interagency screening efforts that may affect students. "Visas Mantis" is the codeword that refers to a screening process designed to look for inappropriate access to sensitive technology. "Visas Condor" is a codeword that refers to a screening process for counterterrorism purposes.

Consular officers generally send an interagency screening request the same day of the interview or the next day. The request is in the form of a telegram that is simultaneously transmitted to the Visa Office and all appropriate federal clearing agencies.

*Visa Issuance*

In most cases, the consular officer makes a final decision whether to issue a student visa at the end of the interview. The applicant is informed of the decision at that time. The consular officer notes the visa decision in the automated system. In the case of a visa denial, the consular officer is required to add his/her reasoning to the system. The officer may also include notes in issuance cases.

If approved, the applicant's passport and approved application form(s) are provided to the clerical staff for visa printing. Normally, the visa is printed in the afternoon or the next day.

*Visa Delivery*

Visaed passports are delivered to applicants in a variety of ways. Some low-volume consulates are able to produce visas while the applicant waits. Other consulates have a designated time to return passports in the afternoon or the next day. Many consulates have introduced a courier system whereby visaed passports are delivered directly to the applicant's home address after several days, and the individual does not have to wait at the consulate.

The Department of State does not have any statistics concerning how much officer time or man-hours an individual visa takes to process. Interview times will vary among applicants, and preparation time will vary due to local conditions.

Once a visa is issued, the student may travel to the United States at any time during the period the visa is valid, although an initial-entry student may not enter the United States more than 30 days before the start of classes.

**Question submitted by Representative Lynn Woolsey**

*Q1. There have been cases at American universities, including incidents at the University of California campuses, where international scholars have had to be detained upon arrival in the United States because there were problems with their paperwork. Through some of the anecdotal information I have received, I have heard of professors and scholars, who arrive without having completed every step of a new clearance process, but they have letters from their universities, inviting them to the Unites States. In some of these instances, the scholars were harshly detained and poorly treated while their visa status was investigated. I am concerned that international students and scholars, whose contributions to American society and education are immeasurable, are afraid to come to the United States. They have heard horror stories about people being handcuffed, detained on wooden benches with a small blanket, and denied access to their luggage or medicines. Rather than potentially face this type of treatment, international students and scholars may choose to study or present their research in other countries. I do not have issue with the fact their entry is delayed until problems are resolved, but I think there should be a protocol for handling these cases in a more reasonable and standardized way.*

*Do officials at American ports of entry have the proper training and financial resources needed to manage detained international scholars in a humane way that encourages them to come back?*

*A1.* The Department of State cannot address the issues concerning procedures at Ports of Entry. That is the responsibility of the Department of Homeland Security.

The Department of State can affirm that we have proactive public outreach programs to ensure that scholars understand that to travel to the U.S. they must have visas appropriate for the type of activity they wish to conduct in the U.S. We also have close working relations with the DHS National Targeting Center (NTC) that supports port of entry inspectors. NTC may phone us to discuss the case of an individual who has arrived with incomplete and inappropriate information. We use replicated data from our overseas posts to help advise NTC about specific cases.

ANSWERS TO POST-HEARING QUESTIONS

*Responses by Robert J. Garrity, Jr., Deputy Assistant Director, Record/Information Administration, Federal Bureau of Investigation*

**Questions submitted by Chairman Sherwood Boehlert**

*Q1. GAO made a number of recommendations to reduce the time necessary to adjudicate visas for foreign students and scholars. Among them, GAO urged the Secretary of State, in consultation with the Secretary of Homeland Security and the Director of the Federal Bureau of Investigation, to develop and implement a plan to improve the visa process, with milestones for pending cases and performance goals and measurements for future cases. What steps are you taking to develop and implement a plan? Specifically, what are you doing to establish milestones and performance goals? How should Congress evaluate whether the planning recommendation is being implemented?*

*A1.* The FBI is participating in the development of the Department of State's (DOS) new visa database. DOS and the FBI have agreed on the process by which electronic visa information will be transmitted between them, and a Memorandum of Understanding is in the final stage of completion. In the interim, DOS submits requests to the FBI on computer disc. This process is highly reliable and has improved processing times.

Additionally, the FBI and DOS, as members of the Intelligence Agencies' Working Group, are reviewing the need for the approval of Visas Mantis by the FBI. In the interim, DOS notifies the FBI of cases requiring immediate attention so the FBI can provide expedited resolution.

The FBI is able to track the receipt and disposition of these requests and will be able to measure the performance improvements expected from the application of these new technological and management methods.

*Q2. Your testimony indicated that the main cause for the long delay times in the FBI's visa security checks are for the cases that require the retrieval of paper records. You also indicated that FBI is moving toward a fully electronic database system. What is the status of your planning and your timeframe for deploying this new electronic information system?*

*A2.* The FBI's Records Management Division (RMD) has planned a Central Records Complex (CRC) that will house the FBI's paper records from all 265 FBI locations worldwide. As a preliminary step in relocating all files, the FBI has initiated a multi-year inventory to account for every file in its records system. Those files due for disposal under the FBI's records retention plan will either be destroyed or accessioned to the National Archives. Those files not due for disposal, such as files that have continuing law enforcement, counterintelligence, or counterterrorism value, will be scanned, processed by optical character recognition programs, and uploaded as electronic records in the FBI's electronic record keeping system.

The FBI is working aggressively to achieve a fully electronic digitized record system. Interim improvements within the FBI, including the development of electronic databases to prevent duplicate work, the scanning of files, and work flow improvements, will reduce processing times. The timetable for completing this effort is contingent on multiple factors, including the personnel resources available in the event of evolving priorities, possible enhancements to technology which may improve efficiency and speed the process, legal considerations related to the use of scanned documents for judicial and administrative purposes, and the financial resources committed to this project (including the funding received for the building of the new CRC, which is a first step to be followed by the relocation of closed files so that files of interest can be scanned for future use as digitized records).

**Questions submitted by Representative Bart Gordon**

*Q1. How common is it for defective or incomplete information regarding Visas Mantis security checks to be provided to the FBI from consular officers?*

*A1.* The FBI's tracking of the visa process does not specifically record errors or duplicate visa requests, so the FBI cannot provide a precise response to this question. However, since DOS began providing information to the FBI on computer disc, the number of duplicates and errors has been minimal.

*Q2. Are follow-up requests to State for additional information a significant factor in determining the time it takes the FBI to perform its security reviews?*

*A2.* No. DOS ordinarily sends the appropriate information in the initial request.

*Q3. Do you believe that consular officers apply too little judgment in requesting security checks for visa applications for students and scholars, thereby placing an unnecessary burden on the system that impairs the FBI from concentrating on applications involving true security threats?*

*A3.* The FBI recognizes that all agencies are attempting to fulfill their missions within the finite resources allocated. Consular officers attempt to discern, through a very limited opportunity for interview, whether or not the visa applicant will have access to those American special technologies that warrant a Visas Mantis name check. While the expenditure of more time by consular officers would enable them to make more precise determinations regarding the need for security checks, reducing the FBI's need to expend resources, the FBI has not evaluated how much additional consular time would be needed or how much FBI time would be saved in this effort.

**Question submitted by Representative Sheila Jackson Lee**

*Q1. Please provide a timeline for a student visa application coming through your agency: who it comes from, what form it comes in, how you process it, what your role is, how many actual man-hours are needed per application for those tasks, how much time the application waits in a queue, and then where it goes from there.*

*A1.* Following is the work flow process with respect to the FBI's review of student visa applications from the date of receipt at the FBI through completion. The statistical information with respect to the steps in that process is derived from a recently completed work process study with respect to FBI name checks.

- Visa applications are received via cables from individual consulates or by disc or facsimile from DOS.
- Requests received by cable or disc are processed on the day of receipt through an automated process. Approximately 80 percent of Visas Mantis are returned to DOS within 72 hours as "No Record" responses, indicating that the FBI has no record with respect to the individual involved.
- When an automated search reveals the possibility of a responsive file, the request is forwarded for manual review. This review is conducted by an analyst within 14–30 days. Each analyst reviews the files related to an average of 33 names per hour. Approximately 10 percent of visas are returned as "No Record" responses at this point, meaning that the file did not, in fact, relate to the individual at issue. Consequently, within 30 days of receipt at the FBI, 90 percent of all applications are resolved.
- The remaining applications are forwarded for additional file review; time in this file review queue averages one week. Among recurring submissions, visas are placed among the highest priorities. (White House requests for name checks with respect to individuals visiting the President have the highest priority. Special requests relating to counterterrorism investigations are also given a higher priority.)
- Processing times at this file review stage are as follows.
  - *Electronic files*—Electronic files are retrieved within minutes. It takes an average of 30 minutes for name check personnel to review a given file or reference.
  - *Paper files located in FBI Headquarters*—Files are retrieved within three to 30 days. File service personnel average 40 minutes per file to locate and retrieve a file. It takes an average of 30 minutes for name check personnel to review a given file or reference.
  - *Paper files located in FBI field offices*—Files are retrieved within five to 90 days. An average of 30 minutes is expended to forward a file request to a field office (phone call, e-mail, or electronic communication). Once a file is located, it takes an average of four to five hours for a field office employee to draft a summary of the file for transmission to name check personnel. It takes an average of 30 minutes for name check personnel to review each summary.
  - *Paper files that cannot be located*—A small percentage of files are not located (the exact number of such files has not been maintained). If a file is not located within 180 days, the appropriate substantive FBI office co-

ordinates with DOS to determine whether the visa request can be resolved without benefit of the file. This is a risk management issue that requires the evaluation of several factors by appropriate FBI and DOS personnel.

An additional six percent of requests are resolved through this manual file review, which takes from two to 60 days to complete. Consequently, after a total of 90 days, 96 percent of the requests have been resolved.

- Review of the files related to the remaining applications (four percent), all of which have been identified as being germane to the requester and as potentially having relevant information requiring review by an analyst from the cognizant subject matter office, is typically completed within a week. If there is no objection to granting the visa, the analyst notifies the name check unit and, within 72 hours, DOS is notified. If there is an objection, DOS is notified by cable sent directly from the analyst. 97 to 98 percent of requests are resolved within 120 days after receipt by the FBI.

# Appendix 2:

## Additional Material for the Record

**United States Department of State**

*Deputy Assistant Secretary*
*for Visa Services*

*Washington, D.C. 20522-0113*

March 8, 2004

Dear Mr. Boehlert:

Thank you for the opportunity to testify before you and members of your Committee on February 25 on various visa-related issues. As indicated in my testimony, we have a strong interest in striking the proper balance inherent in our policy of "Secure Borders, Open Doors," and I am committed to working with all agencies involved in making the visa process both efficient and predictable for those coming to the US for legitimate purposes. While security must be our first priority, we recognize and are determined to preserve the crucial benefits provided by international visitors to the United States. Our universities reap enormous economic and scientific benefits from open exchange across borders.

I would like to take the liberty to amplify on one of the points made during the hearing. You asked whether it was true that visa work was generally performed by junior officers with little experience. While it is true that much of visa work is performed by entry-level officers, the term "junior" can be misleading. For your information, I'm attaching profiles of two recent Foreign Service classes. You will see that the average age of new officers is between 33-34 years old. In addition to going through a rigorous selection process, entry-level officers come with a wealth of experience in both the public and private sector. In the 117th class, for example, previous federal experience includes work at the Departments of Commerce, Homeland Security, Navy, US Air Force, State, and Treasury. In the 116th class, entry-level officers spoke a combined total of 39 languages. These profiles are representative of all incoming Foreign Service classes.

The Honorable
Sherwood L. Boehlert,
Chairman, Science Committee,
United States House of Reprsentatives.

The Department builds on the good judgment and experience of entry-level officers through intensive consular, language, area studies and leadership training at our National Foreign Affairs Training Center. As indicated in my testimony, consular training covers all aspects of visa work, including a portion on the security advisory opinion process where Visas Mantis procedures are discussed. While all entry-level officers are not in the consular cone, all officers assigned to visa jobs overseas are well-trained in immigration law and procedures and interviewing techniques. All understand the importance of visa work and its role in protecting US borders while facilitating legitimate travel.

I hope this additional information will help overcome any misperceptions there may be about entry-level officers who are performing visa work overseas. The Department is committed to providing these already talented officers with all the tools they need to provide quality service to those seeking visas or other assistance overseas. Please let me know if you would like any further information.

Sincerely,

Janice L. Jacobs

Attachments:
As Stated

**One Hundred and Seventeenth Foreign Service Officer**
**Orientation Class Profile**
**January 12 – February 27, 2004**

| | |
|---|---|
| **Gender** | Women: 48<br>Men: 45 |
| **Age** | Range: 23-57<br>Mean: 34<br>Median: 33<br>Mode: 32 |
| **Marital Status** | Single: 54<br>Married: 39 |
| **Place of Residence** | AZ, CA, CO, DC, FL, GA, IL, KY, MD, MI, MN, MO, NC, NE, NY, PA, SC, TX, VA, WA, Cameroon, Canada, Chile, China, Croatia, Guatemala, Madagascar |
| **Place of Birth** | AZ, CA, CO, CT, DC, FL, GA, IL, IN, MA, MD, MI, MN, MO, NC, NE, NH, NJ, NM, NY, OH, OK, OR, PA, SD, TX, VA, WA, WI, Bosnia-Herzegovina, Germany, Jamaica, Japan, Mexico, Philippines, Republic of Korea, Thailand, United Kingdom |
| **Highest Degree Obtained** | BA – 25<br>JD – 13<br>JD/MA – 1<br>MA – 37<br>Ph.D. – 4<br>MLIS – 1<br>MD – 1<br>MS – 3<br>MBA – 7<br>MPP – 1<br>MUP – 1 |
| **Previous Federal Work Experience** | AmeriCorps, Bureau of Citizenship and Immigration Services, Centers for Disease Control, Department of Commerce, DOS, Department of the Navy, Environmental Protection Agency, HUD, Navy Seal, Peace Corps, Policy Advisor, Social Security Administration, Teach for America, USAID, USAF, US Army Intelligence School, US Marine Corps, US Merchant Marines, US Navy |
| **Recent Work Experience** | Attorney, Bartender, Business Analyst, City Planner, Consultant, English Instructor, Freelance text editor, Teacher, Human Resources Consultant, Insurance and Investment Advisor, Interpreter, IT Support, Legislative Aide, Marketing Specialist, Mediator, Mom, Physician, President – Cable and Wireless North America, Professor, Project Manager, Social Worker, Membership Director – Girl Scouts of America |
| **Overseas Experience** | Work: 51<br>Student/Tourist: 67 |
| **Career Track** | Management: 19<br>Consular: 13<br>Economic: 17<br>Political: 23<br>Public Diplomacy: 21 |
| **Languages** | Albanian, Arabic, Bengali, Bosnian, Bulgarian, Cantonese, Czech, Dutch, French, German, Greek, Gujarati, Hebrew, Hindi, Hungarian, Italian, Japanese, Kiswahili, Kiribati, Korean, Kyrgyz, Malagasy, Mayan, Lao, Mandarin, Mongolian, Pidgin English, Portuguese, Russian, Serbo-Croatian, Spanish, Thai, Turkish, Ukrainian, Vietnamese, Wolof |

**One Hundred and Sixteenth Foreign Service Officer**
**Orientation Class Profile**
**November 3 – December 19, 2003**

| | |
|---|---|
| **Gender** | Women: 46<br>Men: 49 |
| **Age** | Range: 23-56<br>Mean: 33<br>Median: 31<br>Mode: 33 |
| **Marital Status** | Single: 50<br>Married: 45 |
| **Place of Residence** | AL, AZ, CA, CO, DC, FL, IL, LA, MA, MD, MN, MO, NE, NH, NM, NY, OR, PA, TX, UT, VA, WA, WI, Bolivia, Germany, Mali |
| **Place of Birth** | CA, DC, GA, IL, IN, LA, MD, MN, MO, NJ, NY, NY, OH, OK, PA, SC, TX, VA, WA, WI, Canada, China, Colombia, India, Iran, Poland, Russia, South Korea, Ukraine, United Kingdom |
| **Highest Degree Obtained** | BA – 27 BS – 10<br>JD – 11 MS – 8<br>MA – 19 MBA – 10<br>MPA – 1 BSFS – 1<br>Ph.D. – 4 MPP – 2<br>MIM – 2 LLM – 1 |
| **Previous Federal Work Experience** | Bureau of Labor Statistics, Department of Homeland Security, Department of the Treasury Food and Drug Administration, Peace Corps, State Department, U.S. AID, U.S. Army, U.S. Marines, U.S. Navy, Voice of America |
| **Recent Work Experience** | Analyst, Assistant Director of Marketing & Events Management, Attorney, Consultant, Deputy Sheriff, Director of Development, ESL Instructor, Health Club Director, Lecturer, Police Officer, Investment Analyst, Marketing Coordinator, Media Relations Intern, Mom, National Security Analyst, Organizational Paralegal, Pastor, President, Production Specialist, Professor, Senior Editor, Software Engineer, Teacher, Tour Guide |
| **Overseas Experience** | Work: 56<br>Student/Tourist: 79 |
| **Cones** | Management: 18<br>Consular: 18<br>Economic: 20<br>Political: 21<br>Public Diplomacy: 18 |
| **Languages** | Arabic, Bengali, Berber, Bosnian, Cantonese, Chinese, Croatian, Czech, French, German, Gujarati, Haitian Creole, Hebrew, Hindi, Hungarian, Indonesian, Italian, Japanese, Kikongo, Korean, Laotian, Lorma, Mandarin, Marathi, Norwegian, Persian, Polish, Portuguese, Punjabi, Romanian, Russian, Serbian, Slovak, Spanish, Telegu, Thai, Urdu, Uzbek, Vietnamese |

# Association of American Universities

February 25, 2004

The Honorable Sherwood Boehlert
Chairman
Committee on Science
U.S. House of Representatives
Washington, DC 20515

The Honorable Bart Gordon
Ranking Member
Committee on Science
U.S. House of Representatives
Washington, DC 20515

Dear Chairman Boehlert and Ranking Member Gordon:

On behalf of the undersigned organizations, we thank you for your strong leadership in examining international student and scholar visa issues that are negatively affecting American science. By your words and your actions, you have demonstrated your awareness that current procedures and policies are hampering the ability of the world's brightest international students, scholars, and researchers to study and work in our country, where they contribute to our nation's science and technology enterprise, our economy, and our security. It is our hope that your work will help to bring about sensible security policies that protect our country while maintaining our nation's scientific and economic leadership.

Much as we feared, today's General Accounting Office (GAO) report on visas for international students and scholars confirms that the visa adjudication process known as Visas Mantis is inefficient, lengthy, and difficult. We believe the current Visas Mantis process is discouraging international students and scholars from making the U.S. their destination of choice. We support the GAO recommendation to develop and implement a plan to improve Visas Mantis.

Unfortunately, there may be new evidence to suggest that the Visas Mantis process is already taking a toll on the future of American science. Earlier this month several higher education organizations jointly surveyed U.S. colleges and universities to determine whether there had been a drop in the number of applications from international students for the fall of 2004 compared to the fall of 2003. While the results of the survey are still being analyzed, preliminary results indicate that applications from prospective international graduate students decreased for 2004. We will inform the Committee of our findings when the analysis is complete.

U.S. colleges and universities are the best in the world and they are a beacon to talented individuals all over the globe. The excellence of U.S. education and research draws hundreds of thousands of students who seek educational and economic opportunity. While they are here they contribute to our nation's continuing educational, scientific, and economic leadership. As you know, graduate students are critical to American science. They are the next generation of scientists, engineers, and business and government leaders. The U.S. has for decades been the world leader in attracting the best and brightest international graduate students, and declining international graduate student applications may be a harbinger of a diminishing leadership role for American science. There should be no doubt that other countries will be happy to pick up the slack.

U.S. colleges and universities may also be the most effective transmitters of democratic values around the globe. At a time when we are engaged in a global struggle against terrorism, and while we must be alert to security threats from abroad, compromising the openness of our colleges and universities by erecting excessive barriers to international students and scholars threatens not only our educational and scientific excellence but our standing as the model for open and pluralistic societies around the world.

*1200 New York Avenue, NW • Suite 550 • Washington, DC 20005 • 202/408-7500 • Fax 202/408-8184*
*www.aau.edu*

While the GAO report did not address the Student and Exchange Visitor Information System (SEVIS), we wish to bring a matter to your attention related to its continued implementation that we believe will prove a new impediment to international students and scholars choosing the U.S. as their destination. We strongly support the implementation of SEVIS. It is the single most important step that the federal government can take to improve its ability to monitor international students and exchange visitors. However, we have repeatedly expressed concern that this system is being implemented before it is fully operational, and in a manner that does not take into consideration the significant barriers it imposes to international educational and scientific exchange.

Currently, the Department of Homeland Security (DHS) is in the latter stages of finalizing regulations that will govern a SEVIS fee collection system. Let me state clearly that we do not object to the imposition of a SEVIS fee. However, we do believe that the fee collection process should be as simple and straightforward as possible, and that fee collection should not become a barrier that makes it difficult for international students and scholars to come to this country. As currently structured, we believe the fee payment process does not meet these conditions. The higher education community submitted comments to DHS detailing its concerns and a copy of those comments is enclosed for your review.

Higher education and science are international activities in which the U.S. has been the undisputed leader. If the U.S. is to remain the world's leader in higher education, science, and technology, we must have a visa system that is secure, timely, efficient, transparent, and predictable; that will permit scientific exchange and collaboration; and that enhances homeland security. We support the federal government's efforts to strengthen homeland and national security through the visa issuance process, and we stand ready to work with you to accomplish these goals.

We thank you again for your leadership on these issues.

Sincerely,

Nils Hasselmo

Nils Hasselmo
President, AAU

On behalf of:

Alliance for International Educational and Cultural Exchange
American Council on Education
Association of American Universities
Council of Graduate Schools
NAFSA: Association of International Educators
National Association of State Universities and Land-Grant Colleges

cc: The Honorable Tom Ridge, Secretary, Department of Homeland Security
The Honorable Colin Powell, Secretary, Department of State
The Honorable John Marburger, III, Director, Office of Science and Technology Policy

Enclosure